THE PART-TIME ARTIST

Stay Creative & Pay Your Bills

By

Céline Terranova

Copyright © Céline Terranova 2019

ISBN: 978-1-798-10804-8

Website: theparttimeartist.com
Email: info@theparttimeartist.com

CONTENTS

Introduction 7
Workbook 11
Chapter One: What Artist Do You Want to Be? 12
    A Definition 13
    Settling? 14
    Balance 15
    Making It 17
Chapter Two: Motivation 19
    Why We Do What We Do 20
        Why Do I Put Myself Through This? 20
        Why We Do What We Do 21
        Inspiration 22
        Staying Sane 23
        Find Your "Why" 24
    Motivation vs Habit 25
        Why Motivation Fails 25
        The Difference Between Motivation and Habit 26

Building a Habit ... 27
What About the Reward? ... 29
What if You Have a Bad Habit? ... 30
What Habit Will You Build? ... 31

Chapter Three: Time Management ... 32
- Organise Your Time ... 33
  - Our Limited Time ... 33
  - Time Planner ... 34
  - Time Stealers ... 35
  - Your Natural Rhythm ... 37
  - Your Time Planner ... 38
- Define Your Goals ... 39
  - Progress in Art ... 39
  - Setting Goals ... 40
  - Goal-Hopping ... 43
  - Finished, not Perfect ... 43

Chapter Four: Energy & Health ... 45
- Energy To Create ... 46
  - Why Do You Need More Energy? ... 46
  - What Depletes Your Energy ... 47
  - Saving Energy ... 48
  - Sleep ... 50
  - Nutrition ... 51
  - Exercise ... 52

- Health and Art ... 54
  - Why is Health Impacting Your Art? ... 54
  - How to Create in These Conditions? ... 54
- Chapter Five: Mental Health ... 56
  - Issues Artists Face ... 57
    - Why is Mental Health a Problem for Artists? ... 57
    - Stress, Burn Out and Guilt ... 58
    - Depression ... 59
    - Anxiety ... 60
    - Never Good Enough ... 62
    - Imposter Syndrome ... 63
    - Rejection and Criticism ... 64
    - Other Issues ... 65
  - Help Yourself ... 67
    - Re-program Your Thoughts ... 67
    - You Don't Need to Suffer to Be Great ... 68
    - Surround Yourself With Positive People ... 69
    - Stop Comparing Yourself to Others ... 71
    - Gratitude ... 73
    - Meditation ... 74
    - Keep Track of the Good ... 75
    - Have a "Me" Day ... 77
    - Ask for Help ... 78
    - Your Strategy ... 79

Chapter Six: Day Job & Money ... 81
The Job That Works With Your Art ... 82
The Job-to-Pay-the-Bills ... 82
What Kind of Job? ... 82
Finding a Job ... 84
How to Survive the Job ... 85
Leaving Work at Work ... 86
When to Quit ... 87
Your Day Job ... 89
Making Money ... 90
Starving Artist? ... 90
Budgeting ... 90
Worries about Money ... 93
Is Money the Root of Evil? ... 94
Spending Money on Your Art ... 95
Making Money from Your Art ... 96
Taxes ... 98

Chapter Seven: Going Full-Time ... 100
Pros and Cons ... 101
My Experience ... 101
Stability vs Freedom ... 102
Do What You Love… ... 103
Who Do You Want to Be? ... 104
Your Artistic Business ... 105

      Your Business Plan 105
      Why? 105
      What? 106
      Who? 108
      When? 109
      How? 110
      Let's Begin! 112

Chapter Eight: Being Happy 114
      Being Happy Now 115
      Keep the Spark 116
      Give Back 117

Conclusion 118

Going Further 120

Acknowledgements 121

Resources 122

INTRODUCTION

Welcome, fellow Artist. My name is Céline Terranova, and I am so happy to meet you!

Being a creative is not always easy. Between the lack of consideration from society in general, the ever-growing costs of living, and the demands of adulthood, it is more and more difficult to find time and energy to create. I know, I have been doing it for twenty years!

I have always wanted to be a writer. It might be a cliché, but I can't remember a time when I wasn't sure I would write a book one day. I was inventing stories from a young age and, as soon as I could fathom what a book was, I knew my destiny was to write one.

The problem was that nobody else believed in that destiny. I was born in Mons, a little town in Belgium where not many people envisaged a career as an artist seriously. Writing was seen as a hobby, not a viable career path, and it was not likely to bring enough money to survive. So instead of pursuing my dream, I studied science.

Science was fun when I was a teenager. I loved learning how things worked and I was pretty good at it. Physics was my favourite because it was logic and fascinating. After high school ("Ecole Secondaire" in Belgium), I began studying for a Bachelor, then a Master in physics, in the same Belgian town.

I did not entirely hate my years at university, but I quickly realised that I was not the most passionate scientist. I still liked to learn, but I yearned for something more creative in my life. This is when I discovered something that completely changed my life: fanfiction. For those of you who don't know what fanfiction is, here it is simply put: it's a story told within a universe created by someone else. The story is usually published in specialised websites, and there's a large community of writers and readers involved. I fell into it hard, writing hundreds of thousands of words in the Harry Potter universe. I pretended to everyone (including to myself) that it was just a hobby, and that I was only interested in science. But really, what I was doing was learning how to write properly. Every story allowed me to progress because I made sure to have a proper, critical system of beta readers, and I dissected all their feedback to improve my craft. Fanfictions were the perfect cover for the secret writer that I was.

After university, I decided to continue working in science and set off to Switzerland to study for a PhD in physics. I was still convinced that writing was nothing more than a passion, and that science was my real career. It didn't go well. I began hating what I was doing, I felt more isolated than ever in a country so far from home, and I had to deal with an abusive boss. Fanfiction was my only respite. I was a different person in that world, and I gained quite a success in my genre. I had several popular websites and forums. I was part of many groups. I was confident and I gave advice. I was "Loufoca" online, and most of the time I preferred being her than Céline.

The tip-off point happened two years into my PhD. I remember that day clearly because it was like a lightbulb had switched on in my mind. After a particularly humiliating meeting with my boss, I realised that I couldn't take the abuse and the frustration anymore. I quit not long after that and came back home to Belgium. It was a hard decision, but it was necessary. I was stuck in a life that didn't fit who I was, and it was time I listened to my intuition. After years of ninja writing, with hardly anybody in my real life aware of my online doppelgänger, I told everyone I knew that I wanted to become a professional writer.

This decision didn't make my life easier, on the contrary. I struggled with everyone's perception of my "failure", my aborted scientific career. I was also unemployed for a long time, depressed and alone, because I was not sure how to go about writing for a living. I moved to London in 2012 to make a new start and because I thought that there would be more opportunities here for me. I applied for a lot of jobs that involved writing. I thought it would be easier to make it as a filmmaker at one point, so I made a short film. I tried many avenues...

... And I ended up poorer than ever before — living off my credit card, not knowing if I'd be able to repay it; creatively paralysed because I didn't just need to write well anymore. I had to write commercially, and it was too much pressure. I constantly second guessed everything I was producing, and nobody seemed decided to give me money for things that I wanted to do. The only paid jobs I landed were awfully boring, with all clients seemingly impossible to satisfy. It put me off trying to make money from my writing.

So I did what a lot of artists do in this situation. I got a day job.

I did many day jobs, in fact, from retail to bar work. And four years ago I ended up, almost by luck, in the theatre industry. Working in a theatre was not something I ever imagined I would do with my life. I started at the bottom, selling ice creams and cleaning the toilets, and I climbed my way up. At first it was just a temporary job until I "made it". I didn't put much effort in, just enough to be paid but nothing more. Then I realised that I could still write when I was not at work. I didn't have to hide that my real passion was writing. And better: I didn't have any pressure to make money out of the writing anymore, as the bills were taken care of by my job. It was strangely liberating.

I built the habit of writing every day before going to work. Writing was not a hobby, it was not secret and it was not worthless anymore. I was progressing as a writer, but I was not killing myself doing it. I had a job that paid the bills and that supported me while doing what I was passionate about. For the first time in my life, I had reached a balance. It was not perfect, but it gave me enough time, money and space to launch my artistic career properly.

Recently, I quit my job to become a full-time artist. It would never have been possible without the years spent perfecting my work-art balance, and without the many inspiring creatives that I have met along the way. Despite what society wants us to believe, I know that there is a way to make art while still ensuring a decent quality of life. There is a way to grow and nurture our talent, without struggling to pay the bills. I've learned how to do it, and you can learn it too.

That is why I wrote this book.

WORKBOOK

To help you along this book, I have designed a companion workbook that you can download **for free** from my website:

www.theparttimeartist.com/helpful-tools

It has space to fill in your own answers to questions I raise in our journey. It's not mandatory, and you might want to make your own notes instead. That's absolutely fine. Use this book the way you want.

At that same address, I have also uploaded some other tools that I'll talk about during the book. They are all free and you can choose whether to use them.

CHAPTER ONE
WHAT ARTIST DO YOU WANT TO BE?

A Definition

What I call a "Part-Time Artist" is an artist who is committed to their art, but has a day job to pay the bills. It is a creative person who perhaps would like to do more for their art, but can't because of their circumstances. It is any kind of artist who has heard the speech about "being realistic" and "choosing a real career", but is still trying to succeed in their art.

On Twitter, I asked my audience if they were able to live from their art. I was wondering if it was a majority who struggled with this, or if most people were making their ends meet with their art. The results were illuminating: ninety percent of the people who responded to the poll couldn't live from their art. Ninety percent! An overwhelming majority. Since I love math (I'm a scientist, after all), I pushed the study further. I created a survey online to gather more data: The Part-Time Artist Survey. My first question was to see if those artists who replied to me had a job, full-time or part-time. There again, the answers were interesting: 54.7% of people had a full-time job, while 12.6% had a part-time job. Two thirds of the people who replied depended on a secondary source of revenue.

From what I can see, a large proportion of artists are Part-Time Artists, at least until they "make it". This is often seen as a transition period, and most artists underestimate how long it might last. Worse, when the situation takes too long to resolve, they can become depressed or assume they have failed.

I'm sorry to say this, but making it can take years, or even decades. Most of the time, it has nothing to do with talent, or the amount of work done. It just takes time.

But weirdly, there isn't much advice about how to live this life split in two, between your art and your other responsibilities. I've interviewed performers who told me that they had never had any advice about how to find a job outside of performing. I've spoken with artists who had never been taught how to do their taxes. And as a writer, I have never seen any advice about becoming self-employed or juggling my professional schedule with writing sessions.

It is clear to me that there is a lack of support, and I hope that this book will be a step in the right direction.

I strongly believe that you shouldn't wait until you "make it" to be happy.

SETTLING?

When I say this to other artists, the first reaction that I usually get is negative. Nobody wants to think that their success is not going to be immediate, especially newcomers. If you are a young artist, perhaps still in school, I am sure you would like to concentrate on making it big - and quickly — instead of designing a contingency plan.

I understand this. When I moved to London, I had quite a lot of savings, and I was sure I would find a job in a film production company, or as a writer, long before my savings were depleted. I refused to consider that it might take a while to get used to a new city and a new language.

I was wrong.

Six months later, my savings were gone and I was forced to accept the first job that came my way to be able to pay my rent. That year, I worked in a retail shop over the holidays. My first Christmas in the UK was spent dealing with angry customers. I do not recommend!

So why did I refuse to think about the practicality of living in a city as expensive as London? Why did I not want to think that I needed a job from the beginning, to give me more time to find the perfect artistic opportunity?

Simple: having a normal job meant that I was settling. Somehow, I was caving to the years of pressure that had made me study science in the first place. It was out of the question. Having a job would have meant that I wasn't trusting myself to make it. It was a proof that I was not going to make it. Having a job, settling to a life that was less that what I wanted, that was a failure. No true artist would settle, ever — right?

"True" artists are the ones who make it quickly, aren't they? They get out of school, get their "big break" and become stars. What you need to understand is that **they** are the exceptions, but unfortunately, they are the ones that everyone hears about. It gives a completely distorted idea of success and how quickly it is supposed to come to those starting out in the creative industries.

In reality, for a majority of artists, it takes time and effort. Finding ways to cope with this doesn't mean that you are settling. Settling means that you are not going to try anymore; that you are giving up. That is not what I advocate. The idea is to maintain your progress whilst building a great life.

It's a balance.

BALANCE

To make this concept clear, I am going to use a video game metaphor. I play video games from time to time. I used to play World of Warcraft, and I enjoyed it. Unfortunately, I didn't have much time for playing. I was maybe playing a few hours a week, maximum ten. In the world of gamers, that's nothing. I was a *casual* player. Casual meant that it was just a hobby for me. I was having fun, but I knew that I would never reach a top level in the game. For that, I would have to commit much more to it.

On the other side of the spectrum were the players who spent a lot of

The Part-Time Artist

time in the game — an insane amount of time, by my standards. Easily over 10 hours per day, probably more. These were the *hardcore* players. They got access to the cool stuff in the game and do the most difficult raids with their guilds. Their progress was unmatchable. They were the people every player envied.

I think the distinction between hardcore and casual can be made for artists, too. There are people who create their art purely as a hobby. For example, I paint Warhammer figures (yes, I play video games, and I paint mini-figures. You can say it, I'm a geek!) I do it from time to time, and it is an artform that I like. I like looking at what other people do, and I follow several accounts on Instagram to learn new techniques. I know some people who sew during their free time, or write, or play an instrument. It's their release, their pastime, their luxury. They are *casual artists*. Casual artists often don't consider themselves artists at all. It is their hobby. Even if they aim to be better at it, it's not the most important thing in their life.

Now, the *hardcore artists*. These are the ones who will not compromise with their art and will spend as much time on it as it needs. They don't care if they are in debt or if others have to support them, because their art is more important. They prioritise their art over their partners, their family, their comfort and their happiness.

I do the NaNoWriMo challenge every year, which consists of writing 50,000 words in one month. During that month (November), I'm a hardcore artist. I write as much as I can, and often other parts of my life suffer because of it. But it's OK, because it's just one month. I know that I could not hold that rhythm for much longer, and I don't want to keep ignoring my responsibilities, my chores, my family, or my friends. NaNoWriMo takes a toll on me every year, and it usually takes the following month for me to recover.

That is the truth of the hardcore artist's life: no matter how much motivation and stamina you have, it cannot last forever. It demands too much of an artist, and it is too difficult to sustain for the long term. I have seen many artists give up because they burn out. They have given everything they could and pushed so hard that they broke. It's not sustainable.

Many artists think that they have to choose between those two lives. Worse, they think that if they are not doing it the "hardcore way", they are automatically failing. I don't agree. I believe that there is a middle ground between casual and hardcore: the ***balanced artist***.

A balanced artist is someone who allocates a sizeable proportion of time to their art, even if they would prefer to do something else. A balanced artist is someone who treats their art as a real career, as a job, as something from which they need to provide results. But a balanced artist is also aware that this is a marathon, not a sprint, and therefore they are careful to also develop the other areas of their life aside from their art.

A balanced artistic life is not without hurdles. There are parts of me that don't want to write every day, that would rather watch Netflix than finish writing my last chapter. There are parts of me that want to concentrate on having a family or building a house, instead of investing my savings in my artistic business. But it is a commitment that I have made to myself, and it is infinitely easier than trying to make it the "hardcore way".

MAKING IT

But first, what does "making it" mean? What is the end game exactly?

What is success?

This is a question that I have asked on Twitter too, and the replies were illuminating. Success — "making it" — was different for everyone. Some people talked about earning a lot of money or being famous, but it was not the majority. For a lot of people, "making it" was a concrete step in their artistic life. It could be something as simple as seeing a book cover with their name on it, or seeing their art being displayed in a gallery. For some, it was more personal, such as aiming to bring their whole family on a nice holiday.

> *"If I inspire someone to be themselves; if I make them understand that it is OK to be gay in this industry. That's how I'll know I have succeeded." — Joseph O'Reilly, Performer.*

> *"My parents will be well looked after. They have given up so much for me to get where I am today. So I'd like to see them being happy in retirement and not working too hard." — Wayne Burke, Performer.*

"Making it" can change with age, too. What you want when you are 18 is usually different than when you are 40. It doesn't mean that you lost your dream on the way or that you are settling for less. It means that you values and your comprehension of the world change over time, and that is not a bad thing.

For some people, being able to become a full-time artist - in other words, being able to live off their art - is the end goal. I will address this particular goal later in the book.

Regardless of what your concept of "making it" is, this book has been written to help you during the transition period, during those months, or years, when you are working towards your goals. And hopefully, during which you are happy!

CHAPTER TWO
MOTIVATION

WHY WE DO WHAT WE DO

WHY DO I PUT MYSELF THROUGH THIS?

Writing is difficult. It might not appear to be, but I can assure you that anyone who has ever tried to write a book has found this to be true. Writing can take an insane amount of time. It took me over nine months to write the first draft of my first novel. The second draft took even longer. That was with writing or researching every day. It was a painstakingly slow process.

Some days, I would do anything, ANYTHING, not to have to sit in front of my computer and write. I have back problems and it can be painful to write. In terms of mental health, writing becomes a rollercoaster that has its ups when a project goes well, and its downs when nothing comes out on the page right.

I have interviewed performers who told me about the anguish of auditions. Actors who have to pay for exorbitant headshots every time they change haircut. Musicians who suffer from tinnitus after years of concerts.

Art, when it is practised at a level above the hobby, is not always fun. And it is not always easy.

What would I give to live a simpler life? I wish I could come home, watch television, enjoy food and perhaps exercise a little, and be happy about it. My life would be easier if I could content myself with work and hobbies and family. There is nothing wrong with it. A lot of people do it, so why not me?

Art is not necessary. Artists don't have to do what they do. We don't have to do anything!

So why are we doing it?

Why We Do What We Do

There is a TED talk from internationally famous coach Tony Robbins that is called *"Why we do what we do"*[1]. In this talk, Robbins defines the six basic human needs: certainty (stability, basic needs met), uncertainty (variety, surprise), significance (feeling special), love (connection with someone or something), growth (expanding capacities), and contribution (helping others). According to him, everything we do is to satisfy one of these needs. For example, if I worked as hard as I did for my day job, it was to satisfy my need for certainty: the insurance that I'll have my salary to pay the rent and the bills.

Now, where does the artistic activity lie?

In my case, I know it is a mix of several of these needs. My writing brings me significance. It gives me a voice and allows me to be someone in this world. It also brings me growth, as every story I have written has made me a better writer and a better person. My writing is always aimed at helping people, even indirectly. I was a lonely child and books helped me feel better. I want to do that for other people. Contribution and love: check!

Tony Robbins says that any activity that fulfils at least three needs becomes akin to an addiction. Not necessarily a negative addiction, like drug use, but an activity that we need to do over and over again. This is how I feel about writing.

---

[1] Tony Robbins, "Why we do what we do" talk.
https://www.ted.com/talks/tony_robbins_asks_why_we_do_what_we_do?language=en

The truth is, I cannot be like "normal people". Watching television, working, commuting, interacting with my friends - all of that fulfils some of my needs, but not in the same way writing does. I feel compelled to write, and to come back to it time and again. Every time I have thought about giving up, something in me prevented me. I cannot stop; it is truly an addiction.

Inspiration

There's another TED talk that I have watched as much as the Tony Robbins one: Elizabeth Gilbert's *"Your elusive creative genius"*[2]. Elizabeth Gilbert is the author of the international best-seller *"Eat. Pray. Love"*. I am, however, more a fan of another book of hers, *"Big Magic"* in which she elaborates on the concepts she discusses in her TED talk. I love it because it addresses the subject of inspiration and where it comes from, and helps us understand — and feel less guilty — about our art. According to her, artists are not the source of creation. We are simply a messenger, a "mule", interpreting messages coming from an unknown origin and transforming it into something that can be communicated to others.

As an ex-scientist and sceptic, this is a concept that at first appeared weird and far-fetched to me. Then I remembered how the idea for my first novel came to me: in a dream. And not just any dream. A dream so powerful that, upon waking up, I had to write down everything about it. At the time I was working in retail on morning shifts, which meant that I had to wake up at 5AM. I am not a morning person, and so waking up so early was pure torture to me. Generally, I was so out of it that I could barely prepare a coffee before leaving for work. But not that day. That day, I was fully awake and aware that I needed to put this idea into writing as quickly as possible. I ended up writing most of the day, during my breaks and in secret on my notebook when my manager couldn't see me. I admit that I wasn't the best employee that day.

---

[2] Elizabeth Gilbert, "Your elusive creative genius" talk.
https://www.ted.com/talks/elizabeth_gilbert_on_genius?language=en

This kind of burst of inspiration has happened only a couple of times in my life. One day, as I was on holiday in Rome, I woke up from another dream in the same state of pure determination. I knew I had to write this one down, too. I spent most of the day writing it, in between visits to churches and walks in the beautiful city.

I know so many artists who have had the same kind of experiences. Suddenly something "clicks", and it is like something higher than yourself commands you to create. I know it sounds mystical, but it's an experience that many artists have lived.

In my mind, my writing is not only an addiction. It is also a message that came to me and that I can't ignore.

STAYING SANE

There is another drive that pushes me to write, and pushes a lot of people to create their art. We live in a world that is difficult to comprehend. My brain is built in such a way that I need to find a reason for everything. I try to find patterns and explanations, where sometimes there are none.

The problem is, the world doesn't make sense sometimes, and it drives me crazy. Writing helps me make sense of what is happening around me. It helps me work out my feelings and what I think about a subject. Sometimes, I don't even know how I feel until I write it down.

I journal quite a lot, especially during dark periods in my life, and it's sometimes the only thing that will help me stay sane. Art can be your shield against everything else that is going wrong, and I know that it is a powerful drive that brings me to the keyboard over and over again.

One of the respondents to the Part-Time Artist Survey puts it brilliantly:

> *"Art IS my coping."* — *Nadi, Mixed Media Artist*

Find Your "Why"

All of this to say that the "why" you are painting / writing / composing / designing / performing is important. So important, in fact, that it is at the root of the whole discussion about motivation that is going to follow. If you are serious about being an artist, if it is not a hobby, then you must have a "why".

Take a few minutes to think about it and write down all the reasons why you do your art. Go into as much detail as you need. Don't hesitate to write down examples. And be honest. If you do what you do to get recognition, to become famous, write it down. Be true to yourself — nobody else has to know! You can use the workbook for this exercise.

Once this is done, pin it on a wall in front of your work station or above your bed. Read it every day. Reflect on it. Add to it, if necessary. These are your strongest motivators. The same way some people pin up the picture of their dream car or their dream house to be motivated to earn enough money to get them, you'll look at these powerful words every day while you work towards your goals.

This is your first step out of the hobby and into your part-time artistic career. Congratulations!

MOTIVATION VS HABIT

Why Motivation Fails

Now that you have found your "why", you probably have a better idea of what motivates you. Motivation is a powerful tool, and it makes you start important and fulfilling projects. The problem, however, comes from continuing these projects once the motivation has dwindled.

There was a study that was published in 2011 entitled, *"Stuck in the middle: the psychophysics of goal pursuit"*[3]. The paper shows exactly the moment where motivation fails: right in the middle of a project. The pattern is eerily similar in most cases. A test subject has a lot of motivation when the project starts, then motivation fails in the middle, to only pick up again near the end.

In writing, we call it the "muddy middle". It refers to reaching the middle of a novel and almost giving up, and at the same time refers to those books that start great and struggle towards the midpoint.

Have you ever started a project, only to stop when the first obstacles showed up? Do you have several works in progress, but have never managed to finish one of them? Do you recognise yourself when I talk about the "muddy middle"?

---

[3] Stuck in the middle: the psychophysics of goal pursuit.
Bonezzi A1, Brendl CM, De Angelis M.
https://www.semanticscholar.org/paper/Stuck-in-the-middle%3A-the-psychophysics-of-goal-Bonezzi-Brendl/67a8837fe8286cdf15207d77acca33d9e3080520

Motivation is not reliable. It will not carry you through the whole process of whatever projects you are working on. Motivation alone can't help you finish a book, a composition, or a painting, and it can't help you go back to it every day. No matter how much you love your current project, there will be days where Netflix is more appealing than your art.

So, you need something else.

The Difference Between Motivation and Habit

Cambridge Dictionary defines a habit as follows:

> *Habit*
> *Noun*
> *Something that you do often and regularly, sometimes without knowing that you are doing it*

Everyone has dozens of habits. Things that we do every day, without even thinking about it: brushing teeth, lacing shoes, putting on makeup, walking the dog... These habits are so ingrained in our personality that we don't question them, and we don't need motivation to do them most of the time.

Usually, a habit is triggered by something: often a time of the day or a particular stimulus. For example, when I get ready for bed, I perform the same actions every day. Brushing my teeth, putting on my pyjamas, applying moisturiser, and so on. The time of the day triggers all these habits, without me making a choice about any of them. Sure, I could skip them, but that would mean making a conscious choice, and therefore using more energy. Instead, it's easier to let the "robot me" accomplish all these actions, so I'm free to think about something else.

Motivation means that we need to be aware of the action we are doing. We spend a lot of energy (or willpower) doing something, and unfortunately we only have a finite quantity of this willpower. A habit, on the other hand, requires almost no willpower. It's much easier to sustain.

BUILDING A HABIT

If you have an ambitious project that you know will take a lot of time and energy to complete, I strongly recommend that you build a new habit around it.

In his book, *"The Power of Habit"*, Charles Duhigg explains the concept of **the habit loop**. A habit is composed of three steps: the cue, the routine, and the reward.

The cue is what I was talking about before: a time of day or a stimulus that will trigger something in your brain, telling it to go into "robot mode". The routine is the actions that we perform in this robot mode. The reward is the proof to your brain that this habit is worth repeating in the future. The best habits have a strong cue and a worthwhile reward.

So, if you want to build a habit around your art, you will have to find a cue that happens often enough, and is specific enough, that it triggers your work on the project. Then a reward that makes it all worth it.

This is something that I have worked out for my writing. My cue is simple: I write at the same time most days. I am careful to have the same kind of routine for everything else, so that writing comes as an automatic follow-up to everything else: I get up, have breakfast, exercise, shower, get ready, and write. Having a specific time of the day for writing is the most efficient and powerful cue that I could get. It's like I'm programmed to write, and if I don't do it I feel lost. As soon as I see the clock on my laptop, it triggers the habit. It makes it much easier to start writing.

I reinforce this main cue with other smaller cues, which other people call "rituals". I put my earphones in and I listen to the radio. I make tea or coffee, I place my notebook near my laptop, I tweet that I'm writing (peer pressure and accountability add to the cue!).

If you can't practice your art every day at the same time, these rituals are even more important. The idea is to trick your brain into going into "robot mode". Recently, I advised another writer on Twitter to listen to the same song every time he started his writing session. It worked! It put him immediately in the mindset for his project. Music is a powerful tool to trick your brain.

Don't disregard your other senses when it comes to creating a cue. This was proved by a Russian physiologist named Ivan Petrovich Pavlov who studied conditioning and made the renowned experiment where a dog was conditioned to salivate when hearing the sound of a buzzer that was associated with food in its mind. Even scent can be a powerful stimulus to your mind.

Some other signals are more subtle. I used to only be able to write during my commute. My days were crazy busy, and only when I was on the tube or the bus did I have time to put down some notes. Religiously, every time I was on public transport, I would get my notebook out and write. All the stimuli associated with public transport were so powerful that I still feel the urge to get my notebook out, years after I built that habit.

So, think about it. What cues can you use to trigger your art? What works every time you've tried it? What time of the day means art for you? Don't hesitate to experiment with these rituals and cues, you might find some that you didn't expect!

WHAT ABOUT THE REWARD?

The reward is there to prove to your brain that it should repeat the loop, that it should carry out the routine when it is triggered by the cue, because it is worth it.

How is it done?

There are several ways of doing this. The first (and most obvious) one is to give ourselves an actual reward. It could be eating chocolate once you're done with your session. It could be watching an episode of your favourite series after a particularly difficult hour. It could be keeping your promise to have fun once you're done with the work. It does work, as long as you are not lying to yourself or giving yourself rewards every five minutes. My brain would not appreciate the chocolate at the end of the session if I gave myself five more every time I finished a paragraph. Similarly, if I promised myself I would play a video game once I wrote 3000 words, but when I reached my goal I kept writing because I was late on my deadline. Next time it won't work because my brain will remember the lie!

Practice being honest and accountable with yourself, the same way you would do with other people. Your reward system should be fair, consistent, and reinforced on a regular basis.

Another way to reward yourself is to track your progress, in a quantifiable way. Let's say you are a performer, and you have decided to train for a particularly complicated show. Track every progress you have made. Prove to yourself that this session was worth it because now you have mastered a given part of the show.

I will talk later about setting goals and how it helps to track your productivity, but at this stage make sure you recognise the progress that you make every day. It is a powerful reward, and often something that stays with you longer than chocolate!

WHAT IF YOU HAVE A BAD HABIT?

A bad habit is difficult to change, and even more difficult to remove completely. Like many people, I used to be a smoker. I was not a big consumer, but enough to make it difficult to quit. The problem was not the addiction to nicotine. The issue was that I had made the habit to take a break regularly to have a cigarette. The cue would be "I need a break". The routine would be going outside and smoke. And the reward would be the five minutes of peace outside.

How did I break it? Nicotine chewing gums helped with the addictive part, but they didn't help at all when I needed a break and reverted to the cigarette. So, when the cue of needing a break came, I changed the routine: I still went outside, and I had quiet moment to myself. I kept the cue, and I got the same reward, but with a different routine.

It goes this way: old cue — new routine — reward.

Let's say, for example, you have developed the bad habit of putting yourself down every time you talk about your art to someone else. It's stronger than you: every time someone asks about your current project, you can't help but point out all the things that are not perfect about it. The reward being the other person probably reassuring you and making you feel better.

In your new habit, the cue remains the same: someone asks about your current project. The routine needs to change to something like, "I can't talk about my work in progress, but I'm enjoying doing it," and your reward will be feeling good about yourself. The more you will repeat this new habit, the more ingrained in your brain it will become.

If you have developed a bad habit linked to your art, know that you will have to work harder to break it. It will take a lot of practice and relapses, but if you do it consistently, you'll see the results!

What Habit Will You Build?

So now, instead of relying on motivation, what habit are you going to build to be able to do your art on a regular basis and finish your projects?

Think "cue": what will to be the stimulus that is going to send your brain into robot mode when you sit in front of your laptop, grab your brushes or warm up your voice? Be specific, and don't hesitate to pile on additional cues.

Then think "reward": how are you going to make your brain understand that it's worth it? How are you going to associate the habit with joy or pleasure? How are you going to know that you it's worth your while to repeat it? Here again, be specific.

Then think "routine": what is it that you do during your work sessions? Associating the routine with the cue and reward is important, because they work best together.

In the companion book, I've provided you with space to fill with your own answers.

CHAPTER THREE
TIME MANAGEMENT

ORGANISE YOUR TIME

OUR LIMITED TIME

Part-Time Artist is a term that came to me when I was thinking about my life so far and how I divided my activities. I thought it was appropriate, as it showed how little time I had for one part of my life or the other.

To be perfectly honest, sometimes it felt depressing. Some days I felt like writing, but I had to go to work. Or I had a great idea, but that's the day I had to do all the chores that I couldn't do during the week. It's so unfair! Why spending so much time doing things that I didn't want to do? Why did I need to be so reasonable? Why did I never have free time for relaxing?

Accepting that I was not a full-time artist was easier some days than others. Sometimes, it felt like I had no time to take a break and re-assess what I was doing because all my time off was spent writing.

Being realistic is frustrating, but necessary. This book won't magically act like a Time Turner and free tons of hours in a day. If I could do that, I would be rich!

What I propose in this chapter is to show ways to reorganise your time to give valuable space to your art. Not stolen moments once in a while, but consistent chunks of time that will help you build a regular habit and make progress.

Time Planner

The best way I've found to free time for writing is to plan the activity the same way I plan appointments. Every Sunday, I make a "weekly planner". It's a basic sheet of paper that shows every day of the week, where I can draw blocks of my activities. You can find an example on the website:

www.theparttimeartist.com/helpful-tools

I start by adding activities to the planner that are fixed in my schedule: work, commute, sleep, appointments. These are the things that take the most time and that I can't change. It used to be particularly useful for my work commitments, because I worked shifts that differed week after week.

Then I add the chores: cleaning, washing, cooking, laundry, even washing my hair (every long-haired person knows that it can take ages!). All the things that I can't escape doing as an adult. These will vary immensely depending on your circumstances. For example, if you are a parent, there are a lot of things associated with taking care of children. Again, they are inescapable, so they need to be planned and accounted for.

Next, I add the "pleasure" things: time with friends and family, time to relax, shopping. These are the times that I set aside to stay sane. They are vital too, and you can't skip them for long before you burn out. Sometimes, knowing that I will be having a drink with friends on Saturday keeps me holding on for the whole week.

These three categories have different colours, making them visually recognisable on the planner.

Once this is done, I look at what's left blank on the planner, and this is where I plan my writing sessions. I add them in a different colour, so I can see them clearly.

One important aspect of this work is that if there's nothing left blank on the planner, I need to reorganise. I want to see my "writing time" colour several times during the week. It has to be fitted somewhere, so I play a game of Tetris to be able to fit it in.

One of the artists I interviewed had her own system:

> *"I put everything in my diary when it comes to singing: to-do's, commitments and training are colour coded pink, hobbies go in green, and going to the theatre goes in blue. I know I like to see two or three each of pink and green things every week, and maybe two or three blues a month in order to be satisfied with my balance."* — Lauren Shields, Singer

This planner system helped me free more time for writing than I ever did before. The most helpful tool is to measure exactly how much time some activities take. I grouped some stuff to be more efficient and allowed myself to be more relaxed when I had a long day at work.

Once it started to become a habit, I reversed the process. I still added fixed activities first, but I added the writing time next, and crammed everything else around it. What you focus on expands. I managed to expand my writing time for several days in a week, with all the chores and family time still there. Just less procrastination — or time stealers!

Time Stealers

Our lives are full of activities that are not essential, but take up a large portion of our time. Television, Netflix, books, commute, video games, social media — they all have the unpleasant tendency to steal our art-making time without us realising.

How do we get rid of them? Can we get rid of them?

I am a writer, and the last thing I want is to stop reading books or watching potentially inspiring films. I love a good video game, and I religiously follow some series on Netflix. Do I need to stop all of these to be a professional writer?

Well… yes and no. If you take your artistic career seriously and want to give yourself enough time to progress, you will have to give up some time stealers, which means that you may not be as up to date as other people in some aspects of culture or news. This can be difficult for many people.

What I found helpful was to plan these activities, the same way I planned everything else. For example, I love reading. I read every genre and style, and I don't plan on stopping. When I had a full-time job, I also had over an hour of commute to kill. Solution found! I read while in the Tube.

I don't have terrestrial television, because I can't stand adverts, but I watch Netflix or Prime only when I eat. Breakfast, lunch, dinner. It gives me a timeframe for programs, and when I'm done I change activity.

Plan your time-stealers so that they don't have as much control on you anymore. Automate when you can. Remove an activity if it doesn't make you happy. I've stopped reading the news in the morning, because each day was more depressing than the last. Instead, I replaced the BBC News application on my phone with one that shows me "positive news". It makes me feel better, and it has less content, so takes less time.

Your Natural Rhythm

Perhaps you feel reluctant to introduce so much planning into your life? Or perhaps you have tried before, but it didn't work?

Planning can make us feel like mindless minions doing everything that is required of us without thinking. And that's not what I mean when I talk about tricking your brain into going into "robot mode" to build a habit.

A good planner should always include some flexibility. Plans change, days are different, spontaneity is important. You are a human being and you will not always be able to do everything you have planned. That's absolutely fine! I don't always do everything that's on my planner. Sometimes I say I will write a thousand words, but I get up with a bad case of "I need a day off" and don't manage to do anything.

It happens. It's OK. The most important is that you mostly do what you have planned, because at the end of the week that's when you will see the progress. You skipped one art-making session? Not a problem! You skipped all of them? Maybe something is wrong.

Ask yourself the question: does it feel natural for you to do this activity at this particular time? Let's say, for example, that you are a morning person. You will probably not be able to create in the evening, no matter how much time you free up. I am not a morning person, so the most natural time for me to write is in the late afternoon. It is therefore important for me to schedule a writing session during that time of the day. I am also useless unless I have my coffee and shower in the morning. Therefore, I always plan them first.

The time planner is there for you to adopt a schedule that corresponds to you!

Your Time Planner

Take some time to think about the week to come on a day that makes sense to you. I usually do it on Sundays evenings, but it might be that it's easier for you to do it on Monday mornings. Think about the activities that you will have to do this week. Use fun colours to illustrate the different categories.

Plan your creative time. Even if at first you can only give yourself half an hour per week. Highlight those times and make your family aware that you will be creating during them.

Be extremely protective of those creative sessions. Don't let the time stealers win. Don't let other obligations remove them completely.

Once you know how much time you will have, you can start setting goals.

DEFINE YOUR GOALS

PROGRESS IN ART

Before I go into detail about how I set goals for my writing, I think it is important to talk about the notion of progress. How do you know you have progressed in your art? How do you know you are a better artist?

Depending on your field, progress will look extremely different.

For a writer, progress can be finishing a piece, a chapter or having a book published. It is usually easy to see the progress: we can measure the number of words, for example. If you are a painter or a composer, you can also see tangible progress with what you create; how many pieces or how advanced they are. Progress is quantifiable.

However, how do you measure your progress if you are a performer, if the shows you do entirely depend on someone else choosing you? Do you measure the number of auditions to which you are invited? Do you measure your progress with the new skills you acquire? Do you count the number of classes you go to?

Tricky, isn't it?

In business, "KPIs" are used to measure progress. This stands for "key performance indicators", and they are a set of ways an organisation can measure progress or assess if success has been achieved. These are decided by the managers, the shareholders or the CEOs, in alignment with the organisation's mission statement, vision or strategy, and are the areas where they know performance needs to be monitored. They can be linked to revenue directly (e.g. how many sales a department makes) or indirectly (e.g. how many accidents happened). Regardless, they are ways for a company to measure how they are doing.

The key here is to choose your own KPIs, the measures that make sense **for you** and **what you want to achieve**. One of them could be how many followers you have on social media. Another could be how many new techniques you learn in a year, or how many completed projects you achieve in six months.

Take some time to think about your KPIs. Write them down and be as precise as possible.

Setting Goals

Continuing with my business analogy, the way we set goals can be summarised with an easy mnemonic: SMART. You might have heard of this concept in your day job.

It stands for: Specific. Measurable. Achievable. Relevant. Time-bound.

Specific
There is no point in setting goals if you don't have them clearly defined. Go back to your "why" that you wrote earlier. What do you want to do and why? If it is a big goal, divide it in smaller, more manageable goals, and be as detailed as possible.

For example: I want to be a published author. OK, that is the big global goal. Divided into smaller goals:
- Outline the novel,
- Write the first draft,
- Edit/write the second draft
- Work with an editor for the third draft
- Polish until it is ready
- Write a query letter and a synopsis
- Make a list of agents to query to
- Query until I received a "yes"

- Select an agent
- Work with the agent to make the book the best possible
- Let them query publishers
- Work with a publisher to make the book become real

Specific goals can also be peripheral to your art. Building a website is a valid and specific goal. Writing a certain number of blog posts, too. Or giving classes about your art, or reading reference books.

Measurable

You need a way to measure your goals, and determine if you are achieving them. Think about your KPIs: how do you measure your progress? That's how you set your goals. Don't think in terms of a vague goal, think in terms of something you can measure.

For example, if your big goal is to be in a West End or Broadway show, your measurable goals could be to go to three classes a week, apply to ten jobs a month, and take a least one singing lesson a week.

Achievable

Is your goal realistic? It is always good to reach up, but if you overestimate what you can do, it will have the opposite effect. Unrealistic goals are a paralytic. If you give yourself the task of creating ten paintings in a day, there's every chance that you will end up doing nothing because the task will be too daunting to even start.

Think about what is realistic, what is possible, and check if your goals meet these criteria.

Are your goals entirely dependent on someone else? I know that, as artists, we depend on the approval or choice of other people at some point, but this is out of your control and should not be part of your goals. Goals should depend on you, for the most part. Don't think, "my goal is to get an agent," but instead, "my goal is to query twenty agents by the end of the year". The choosing comes as a result of your actions. This is called your "sphere of control", as opposed to the "sphere of concern" which is everything outside of your direct influence. Make sure your goals stay within your sphere of control.

Relevant

Relevant goals means goals that make sense for you and your artistic career. This is to make sure that the goals align with your values and why you create.

Is it the right time? Is it too soon in your career to think about it right now? Is it the wrong season to concentrate on this goal? Is it really about your artistic career? Or is it a vanity goal that won't bring your further? Social media, for example, can be useful for your career, or not, depending on your field. So, is it relevant to spend time building your profiles?

<u>Time-Bound</u>
Your goals need to have a deadline. This is where you will link to the work we did previously with your time planner. Here's how I do it: at the beginning of the year, I set yearly goals. Some call them New Year's resolutions, but I don't like this term because it has negative connotations.

Then, I "place" these goals on my year. For example: if I want to write a brand new book, I say, "Between June and October, I'll do the outline, then I'll write the first draft in November-December". I have a timeline on my notice board that says exactly that. This timeline can evolve during the year, because I know that sometimes life happens and I can't achieve my goals in the time I had planned. Sometimes new projects arise, so I may need to carve some space for them.

Once I do that, I check my weekly planner, and I set my goals for the week to come, knowing what I need to achieve in the month. Some are easier to set than others. Let's say it's November, and I do NaNoWriMo — that means I have to write 1667 words per day. As well as that, I need to create a new website. I can say, "Next week I will create two pages of my website". Or if I'm not sure of what to do yet, "These two hours that are free on Sunday, I'm going to spend them on my website". Repeat every week.

Always set a deadline for your goals, or you will not have the same drive to accomplish them.

Goal-Hopping

Now that you have your goals, I want to talk briefly about a problem that most artists have to face: goal-hopping. Some of you might know it as "shiny object syndrome". It means abandoning one project for another one, because the new project seems more attractive than the one you are currently working on.

The problem with goal-hopping is that you might tend to start a lot of projects, but never finish them. Not only do you lose the motivation for your work in progress, but you also get a lot of motivation for the new thing, because you haven't faced any obstacle in it yet.

Sometimes it is worth taking on a new project before something else is finished. I am writing this book between two rounds of editing of my current novel, because I needed a break. What I did, however, was to plan carefully, with tight deadlines, and a plan to go back to the novel once the first draft of this book is finished.

Most of the time, however, I have to say no to a new project or a new inspiration that is not polite enough to wait for its turn. It's heartbreaking sometimes, but you have to be realistic. Your time is limited and you can't take on board everything at the same time. You have to **prioritise**.

Prioritising can come in the form of planning that new shinny project in a month or two, when you are done with what you are doing currently. Or even giving it to someone else, because you know you'll never come around to do it. Rarely, it can mean giving up your current project for the new thing, but this should be a rational decision, not made on impulse.

Finished, not Perfect

When we talk about goals, there are some that are ongoing, like taking a class every week, and there are some that can be finished, like building a website.

Finishing is extremely important when you are an artist, and especially if you are starting out. The number one time waster for many artists is not television or internet or procrastination. It's perfectionism.

One of the artists I interviewed, Juan Carlos Porcel, showed me a brilliant video[4] from Jake Parker, comic book illustrator and creator of the popular Inktober challenge. In this video, he talks about the artist's need for perfectionism and that it gives us an excuse to never finish a project.

One thing is important for you to know: everything that you will create will be imperfect. You will never reach the perfection that you want. You might reach the level of "good enough", or "not bad" or "I'm actually proud of this", but nothing will ever be perfect. The first things that you finish will probably be pretty rough, maybe even quite bad. That's OK, because you will learn from the experience and go on to the next thing. And they might still be bad, but slightly better. And the next ones will be better, and so on.

But to progress and to go to the next project... guess what? You need to finish it, to put an end to it, to give yourself a deadline after which you will stop fiddling with it and go for the next thing.

So, get your goals, do your projects, and finish them!

---

[4] "Finished, not perfect", video from Jake Parker on Youtube: https://www.youtube.com/watch?v=lRtV-ugIT0k

CHAPTER FOUR
ENERGY & HEALTH

ENERGY TO CREATE

WHY DO YOU NEED MORE ENERGY?

In the Part-Time Artist survey, one of the questions was, "What is your biggest problem as an artist?" The majority of the answers were a variation of, "I'm tired all of the time, I have no energy for my art".

I can identify with this. I often joke that I'm an old lady, because that's how I feel most days. My back hurts constantly, I don't sleep well and I am tired ALL. THE. TIME.

Fatigue is so widely spread worldwide that we don't pay attention to it anymore. It's normal. It's what being an adult means, right?

This becomes a problem when being tired prevents you from performing your art the way you would like to. Who hasn't given up on doing their art because they had an awfully busy day and are too tired? Setting goals and giving yourself a realistic time to achieve them will count for nothing if you are too tired to do anything when you are supposed to work on your art.

If you want to be a balanced artist, you will have to learn how to manage your energy levels for your art sessions. And it is more difficult than it sounds!

WHAT DEPLETES YOUR ENERGY

Before I delve into this section to help you have as much energy as possible, I need to ask you a simple question: where do you put most of your energy?

Energy is a weird thing. It seems finite. We feel sometimes completely depleted, then something happens and suddenly we get a burst. I remember when I received an email announcing that I would be published in a magazine for the first time. It was at the end of a shift at work. I was craving my bed, exhausted, and in a bad mood. I didn't want to talk to anyone or hear anything. Then I checked my phone… and suddenly my whole body changed. Suddenly my energy levels spiked. I was energised again, as if the whole day hadn't happened. I almost ran all the way up to my office (on the fourth floor, no lift!) to announce the good news to my colleagues. I felt like I could conquer the world. What a difference! Equally, I sometimes get up ready for anything, and one piece of bad news drains me.

There are some experiences that are more likely to suck all our energy than others. If you have the same type of personality as me, you might give everything you can to every task you start. You can't function unless you give one hundred percent to the task at hand. The problem is: that is tiring!

You might also face a situation at home that requires all your energy. Maybe you are a parent or a carer, or maybe you are going through a rough patch at home. Perhaps you are simply too spread out. You might be trying to do too much and don't give yourself some rest, or you can't have the rest you need because of issues such as insomnia.

Before we start this work, you need to identify what depletes your energy. You might not be able to change these activities, but it is important that you are aware of it. Make a list of all the activities and situations that demand a lot from you. Be specific. "Working" is not enough. Try "this particular activity at work".

Be specific with the type of situations that you find are the most tiring for you, and how your personality might affect them. For example, introverts might struggle to keep their energy when they are surrounded by a lot of people. Similarly, extroverts might feel more tired when they spend a lot of time alone. The idea here is not to judge but to know yourself as well as you can.

SAVING ENERGY

Now that you have your list, it's time to see if there is anything you can do about it. Observe each element individually. Are they entirely necessary? If you can eliminate some things, that is already a win. For example, a few years ago I was doing my food shopping the way many people do, by going to a physical supermarket. Since I don't have a car and I've been battling back problems for years, it was quite an ordeal. When I realised that it was so time and energy consuming, I switched to home delivery. It saved me feeling run down and helped with my back problems. Plus, weirdly, it also saved money because instead of grabbing everything that I saw while tired and frustrated, I had a proper list and budget.

This is a small example, and of course it might not apply to everyone, but what I want you to take from this is that you CAN eliminate some energy-drainers, or replace them with something that will make your life easier. It's not a bad thing!

Now, of course, eliminating is not always possible. You can't eliminate your job, taking care of your kids, or doing some chores. The trick is to make sure you put in a reasonable amount of effort into them, without burning out.

Your personality will play a big role in your energy management. I suspect that most of the people reading this book have a personality that allows them to do great and fantastic things. Determination, a hard working attitude, giving a hundred percent to everything. And whilst it is great for your art, it's not always a good thing when you exhaust yourself for everything else.

I am the kind of person who used to forget to eat at work when I was too busy concentrating on my tasks. I never took breaks. I cared about every task immensely, and took everything that went wrong as a personal failure. There's a lot to unpack there, and I will go into more detail in later sections on self-esteem and mental health. However, it's no coincidence that I used to feel too tired to write all the time. I was giving my energy away every day, without thinking about what was most important. Nowadays I am more conservative with my efforts. It doesn't mean that I slack off; I am careful to eat, drink and take breaks, and prioritise things instead of trying to do everything at once.

Are there any elements of your list that could use less effort, without losing any of the results? Perhaps some chores can be done less in depth? Or could you allow yourself to do something imperfectly for once?

Add a sentence next to these elements. Write either "ELIMINATE" and the alternative, or "REDUCE" and a way in which you can spend less energy on this activity.

SLEEP

Now that we have managed to reduce the energy spent on other activities, let's focus on ways that you can increase your available energy each day. The first way to do this is to sleep well.

Is this obvious? Absolutely. Do we all do it? Hell no!

I am a primary culprit when it comes to not prioritising sleep. I am the kind of person who is tired all day long, and when it comes time to go to bed, I always have something better to do instead. When I wake up, tired and grumpy, I always tell myself: "Tonight, I'll go to bed earlier".

I am quite good at lying to myself, as you can see.

Aside from not going to bed early enough, I also don't have a good quality sleep and I don't recuperate properly. I used to have terrible insomnia when I was a teenager. I could not fall asleep at all most of the time due to big stressful events happening the next day, like an exam. Now I have the opposite problem: I fall asleep relatively easily, but I wake up several times during the night. I told you, I'm an old lady!

This interrupted, short, sleep is extremely bad. I've been putting a lot of effort lately to correct it, because I am aware that I can't continue at the same rhythm, without having a good rest on a regular basis.

There are several things that you can do to improve your sleep. If you are a night owl like me and you never want to go to bed, only to wake up the next day cursing your past self for not sleeping sooner, there are solutions. There are apps and add-ons that can "force" you to stop using your phone or computer after a certain time. You can force a new habit, or routine, that starts at the same time every day and results in you being in bed by a certain time. You can observe the activities that keep you awake and choose to do them at a different time.

If you sleep badly like me, there are also things that can be done. I have recently invested in a high quality mattress and pillow. It made a big difference! I also use earplugs if my upstairs neighbours decide 6AM is an acceptable time to vacuum their flat. My back pain — one of the biggest source of my sleep problems — is a work in progress.

It might be a good idea to discuss your sleep issues with your doctor, too. Sometimes a bad sleep can be caused by an underlying issue such as sleep apnea, and it is important to detect these on time. In the UK, there are sleep clinics and insomnia treatment available with the NHS. This might also exist in your country.

Do you get your solid eight hours of sleep, or do you have to survive on much less? Not everyone has the same needs, of course, but it is valuable to take some time to think about how you can improve this area. Your art will be better if you are rested and ready to dig deep!

Nutrition

Another source of energy is what you give to your body. Again, this might be obvious, but whoever hasn't gorged themselves on a juicy McDonalds throws the first stone!

I was lucky to be raised in a house where both my parents valued healthy eating. I had plenty of fruits and vegetables readily available, and not much in the way of sweets or unhealthy snacks. It was a nightmare as a kid, when I always wanted more crisps or chocolate, but it has given me a good reference for what a healthy nutrition is.

I became an adult, and suddenly I could eat whatever I wanted without any check. You bet I enjoyed it! Until three years ago, I was eating pretty badly — lots of ready meals, lots of meat, lots of junk food, and probably too much alcohol. Blame the crazy work schedules!

Three years ago, however, I decided to make a big change. I revamped my diet and went back to the basics that I learned from my parents, full of fruits and vegetables. I drastically reduced my junk food consumption, and limited meat. Making that big change had a huge impact on my energy levels and my health in general. I had lots of stomach and digestion problems, and they have been reduced. It also helped me feel more energetic during the day, and when I get sick, it rarely knocks me out completely, as eating more healthily has bolstered my immune system. I used to take days off for a simple cold, and any illness would drag on for weeks. That doesn't happen anymore, and I can feel it every time I fall back into old habits: suddenly, I'll feel sluggish and depressed.

A good way to start is to observe what you eat on a daily basis. Perhaps make a list and see if the food you ingest serves you or not, and how it makes you feel afterwards. Does it give you the necessary vitamins, proteins and fibres that your body needs? Could you do better? Could you cook more often instead of buying takeaways? Could you choose to have fruits as snacks? Swap sugary drinks with water?

The idea here is NOT to put you on a diet. This is not the subject of this book, and I am not a dietician or a doctor. I am unable to recommend what you should eat or not. I am simply conscious about what my body absorbs and it pushed me to design better meals to have a better outcome.

Ultimately, the goal is to feel better so that you can give more of yourself to making art. Try eating healthier for a week or two and see how you feel. And don't forget to add this meal prepping to your weekly planner, to make sure you allocate the right amount of time for it.

Exercise

Exercise is another thing that we all know we should be doing… and that most of us don't do enough. I'm one of the lazy sods who'd rather watch TV than go out for a run or hit the gym. The paradox is that when I DO do these things, I feel a hundred times better afterwards. I feel more sharp, energetic, and happy.

Studies have shown that even a moderate level of exercise every day can make a big difference for your health, including your mental health because of the dopamine released during the exercise. It's almost as dangerous to be completely sedentary as it is to smoke! So many illnesses and problems can be resolved by making sure we get enough activity during the day.

Then… why are we not doing it?

If you remember the discussion about motivation vs habit, I spoke about how motivation doesn't help in the long term. It takes a lot of motivation to drag yourself to the gym. A lot. If at the beginning you have enough motivation, there will come a time when willpower alone is not enough. You've used it all up on other things, perhaps even on doing your art, and you stop going.

How do we combat this? The same way we combat procrastination: creating a habit. Due to my back problems, I was forced into performing stretching and core-building exercises every morning. I didn't have a choice at first, because I was in so much pain that I could not stand up properly without stretching first. Then a weird thing happened: even when I was not in pain, I still did it! It became a habit. This simple, 10 minutes-long series of exercises became part of my morning routine.

You can do this, too. The mistake that most people make when it comes to exercise is to start too big. Begin with a reasonably small amount of time and a few exercises that you can do every day. If you can do this at home, for free, it is even better. Some people start with a 10-minute run. It's not silly, it's part of building the habit.

Since I've started doing my stretches every day, I've felt more in control and more energetic. It was not an immediate change, but it was an improvement. If you are looking to have more energy, think about incorporating more movement in your life. Even something as simple as taking a walk, or investing in a standing desk, could help. And don't forget: add it to your weekly planner!

HEALTH AND ART

Why is Health Impacting Your Art?

In the Part-Time Artist survey, several people talked about health problems, disabilities and long-term conditions that impacted their art.

I have mentioned several times my back problems, and you might also have seen me lamenting about it on my blog or on Twitter. I have a herniated disk and from time to time, the nerve next to it gets inflamed. If I carry something too heavy or twist too much when it is sensitive, my back muscles can go into spasm and I get blocked, to the point where I am unable to walk or move properly, let alone write.

The truth is, it sucks! If your body decides that you cannot do anything creative today, you will not be able to work. Or walk. Or do anything without pain. I am lucky that it is not permanent and that I have more good days than bad ones. I know that some people are not so lucky.

The problem with health issues is that they tend to physically prevent you from doing your art. It doesn't matter if you have time, or if you have the energy. If you can't do some movements or if you are in constant pain, you can't create.

How to Create in These Conditions?

We are not all equal when it comes to our health, and therefore we are not all equal with what we can do for our art. Some people will be able to do more and others less.

When it comes to my back, I plan my schedule around it. If I have a bad day, I will purposely write less to not aggravate the situation. If I'm feeling better, I catch up. If I am in so much pain that hitting a keyboard is simply impossible, but I still have the energy to create, I use dictation.

If you have a health issue or a disability that impacts your creativity, what are the ways around it? Can you schedule your creative sessions around it? For example, if you are in more pain or more tired in the evening, perhaps you can plan all your sessions in the morning? If you know there's a time of the month or the year where it is more likely to flare up, maybe you can plan fewer goals around that time. Are there tools that you can use to work around it?

Only you can know what will be best, but I encourage you to envisage your condition as one more thing to take in account in your life, one more obstacle, the same way having a job to pay the bills is.

CHAPTER FIVE
MENTAL HEALTH

ISSUES ARTISTS FACE

Why is Mental Health a Problem for Artists?

First of all, artists are not the only ones with mental health issues. According to statistics[5] from the Mental Health Foundation, every week one in six adults will experience symptoms of a common mental problem. This includes anxiety and depression. Worse, one in five adults have considered taking their own life at some point. According to the same research, some groups are more at risk, for example young adults.

However, artists through history have suffered from mental health problems. Famous examples such as Vincent Van Gogh or Sylvia Plath come to mind, and creativity has long been associated with depression, anxiety and suicidal thoughts.

It is difficult to pinpoint the exact reason why artists are more likely to develop mental health issues, but I strongly believe that it has something to do with the poor remunerations of artists and the lack of consideration for their work, in addition to our often over-active brains that never switch off. Depending of what kind of artist you are, or what country you live in, you might not have access to any kind of support. For others, help is there but restricted because too expensive or too far.

---

[5] Statistics on mental health from Mentalhealth.org.uk: https://www.mentalhealth.org.uk/publications/fundamental-facts-about-mental-health-2016

I also think that there's a prejudice against artists who say they suffer from depression. We are seen as "drama queens" or "snowflakes" by a large part of the population. A lot of people can't understand that sometimes distress comes from the exact thing that we are doing, the dream that we are pursuing. You might even feel pressured to be "normal" in your day job or with your family, to prove that your art is to be taken seriously. There's also something to be said about not having the time for any self-care, because we are too busy creating, or putting an insane amount of pressure on ourselves to succeed.

I am not a mental health specialist or a psychologist, but I have had my share of mental health issues and my goal with this chapter is to talk about the things that helped me, hoping they will help you too.

Stress, Burn Out and Guilt

I am a high-achieving workaholic. I cannot do anything at less than a hundred percent. I aim to do everything perfectly and I feel immensely guilty if I don't manage to complete everything I had planned.

To give you an idea of how far I get: I blocked my back a couple months ago, while I was still in my day job. I was unable to walk, and needed help to even get out of bed. Needless to say I couldn't go to work and had to call in sick. It made me feel awful! I never called sick, even when I should have. I felt so guilty at letting down my colleagues, though there was nothing to be guilty about.

Sometimes, guilt can come from your circumstances and from choosing art over other things:

> "There's never going to be a correct way of doing things. You are always going to miss some parts of your life. I feel like a terrible dad when I'm at work, and there are times when I feel I'm not doing the best at work because I'm so tired from what I'm doing at home." — Wayne Burke, Performer

Guilt is a powerful feeling that can get you out of procrastination, but it can also run you down. Until last year, I used to only have one day off a week. I worked all six other days, Monday to Saturday. With only

Sunday off, I would have to cram in everything that you would normally do on a weekend in one day: chores, seeing friends, family, resting. I would also be writing most Sundays. Except that some Sundays, I couldn't do it. I was too tired, too busy with other stuff, too run down. And I would feel guilty — can you believe it? My only day of rest, how dare I not use it to write? The truth is, I find resting difficult. I can't do nothing for long before feeling extremely uncomfortable. Guilty. Down.

When you add this to a stressful day job, you get: burnout. Burnout is a state where you feel exhausted, overwhelmed and helpless, mentally and physically. It's not the passing fatigue, it's something that continues on even if you think you've slept enough. It makes you think that everything is hopeless and that you'll never feel better.

Burnout is insidious. You might not even notice it is coming until it's too late. You feel stressed, you can't sleep or you can't get up in the morning, you don't eat well, you feel like you are useless at work or in your life, you feel detached from any consequence your actions could bring. It's not fun.

When you are a Part-Time Artist, you effectively have a second job, which means that you are more at risk of burnout if you do too much on one side or another. Stress is often compounded by the responsibilities you have on both sides, and you probably get less rest time than you should. Burnout is a real danger and you need to be aware of it.

Depression

I rarely talk about my own periods of depression. Years later, it still feels taboo, like something I did badly. Most people who were close to me at the time probably did not see how bad it got, because I was a champion at hiding it.

It all started after I quit my PhD after more than two years of mental abuse from my boss. I left Switzerland and my first ever flat, to go back to Belgium and live with my parents, in the same room I had as a teenager. I had been the talented scientist who had had a job even before graduating, who had moved abroad to a beautiful country. And I came back a failure. My self-esteem, that had already been severely diminished by the abuse I suffered, went down even more at that point. I had to be so strong for so long, on my own against a boss who was a monster, that I couldn't cope anymore. My mood collapsed.

In six months I went from an independent and happy person to a shell of myself, only able to fool my entourage because of a large amount of St John's Wort eaten like sweets. Then I turned 25 and I knew I had to do something, otherwise I would fall further and I would not be able to get out. It took a whole year of therapy and difficult recognition of things that had gone wrong, even before the abuse, to feel better.

To this day, I am still ashamed of having fallen so low, and I am still worried that some people I love might read this and confront me about what happened.

The truth is, depression is common, especially among artists. You might have suffered it already and you might have recognised yourself in my story. Some artists depict it brilliantly in their books, painting, dances. More people need to talk about this experience, and the more we do, the less ashamed we will feel. More importantly, if you are experiencing similar symptoms, it is worth discussing them with a doctor.

Anxiety

At the end of last year, I was diagnosed with an anxiety disorder. Whether it was a consequence of my personality or of the things that happened to me, I don't know. I just know how it feels. The panic that sets off from a specific trigger. The images in my head that take complete control. The whispers in my mind that turn every thought into a negative.

I was lucky to find a great therapist who worked with me on this anxiety and helped me through difficult times where I had anxiety attacks. My therapist advised me to find a name for my anxiety, to find a persona for these negative thoughts that pop into my mind all the time.

I decided to call him Ralph.

Ralph is a miserable sod who sees everything negatively. And he's powerful, very powerful. The kind of character who can overwhelm you. When Ralph is active, it's like he steals half of my brain. I can still function, and most of the time I look "normal", but underneath the surface I'm running the darkest scenarios you could imagine.

Imagination is a fuel for anxiety, which means that artists can build lively and believable stories to validate dark feelings. Sometimes, this anxiety can be used as a source for our art. This book is born from my anxiety, from all the dark feelings I've had in the past ten years. It's my way of doing something about it, to channel this anxiety into something productive.

Sometimes, though, anxiety can be a paralytic. It's the voice that imagines all the bad things that will happen if you succeed or if you fail. Or if there is a zombie apocalypse. I'm not even kidding. My brain imagines seriously every possibility, no matter how unlikely, and tortures me with them. It has prevented me from writing before, and I have had to learn to recognise the signs that Ralph is in charge.

I talk to Ralph sometimes. I ask him to leave me alone. I agree to have a break if he's too annoying, and I coach him, remind him of all the reasons why what he says is wrong. I don't think I'll ever be rid of Ralph, but we have learned to cohabit together in my mind.

I know I'm not the only one doing this. My editor, Vicky Brewster, calls her anxiety "Gremlins":

> *"Gremlins can dress up as real people and lie to you, and they can whisper things in your head, so if my brain is making me feel lousy I check with someone else what the gremlins are saying, and they can tell me if it's true or not."*

Never Good Enough

Low self-esteem is at the heart of many mental health problems. It is a big problem for artists especially, who place so much of their self-value in their art. In the Part-Time Artist survey, I asked "What is your biggest fear?" A lot of people replied, "Never being good enough."

That fear is paralysing. If I'm not going to be good enough, it's not worth starting. If my project is not good enough, I'll keep correcting it until it is perfect. Maybe I'm not talented enough? Maybe I have started too late? Maybe I don't give it enough time?

These thoughts are other ways of expressing the fear of not being enough. It's another way to say, "I am not enough. No matter what I do, I will never be enough." It's a vicious circle, because our art is an extension of ourselves, and therefore our deepest thoughts about ourselves apply to it too.

Years of this internal monolog can be extremely destructive. Art is made to be shared with other people. Whether it is filmmaking, dancing, drawing, sculpting or video game design, you probably want other people to see your project at some point. But if your brain keeps telling that you are not good enough, you risk never taking the leap to share all the incredible things you have done with other people.

Imposter Syndrome

Building on not feeling good enough, there is a consequence that is slowly getting more recognition but was taboo until recently: feeling like an imposter. Let's say you have written a couple of short stories, and you had a few readers who liked them and are asking you for more. If you secretly think that these stories were not good enough in the first place, a disconnect is created. There's the thing that other people see, and there's the real you, with flaws and doubts and imperfection. How can these people want to read me? Don't they see I'm a fraud? Don't they see I have no idea what I am doing?

Or let's say you have been cast for a great show as a dancer. Objectively, you know they chose you for your talent, for your skills, for what you presented at the audition. Except that you don't feel any confidence in those. You may think that they might have made a mistake, and that at any moment you will be discovered. What if I make a fool of myself in front of an entire audience? What if the director realises that I am not good enough and fires me?

This is one of the most paralysing and stress-inducing fears that can plague an artist. It doesn't go away with external validation. On the contrary, it is made worse the more successful you get.

There are many studies on the subject, one[6] arguing that women are more impacted than men, another one[7] (more recently) arguing the exact opposite. To me, it doesn't matter, because I have seen imposter syndrome in many people, men and women.

The feeling of being a fraud can stop you from even trying to do something with your art. It can stop you from putting yourself out there and from enjoying the success you get from it. Worse: it can turn into depression and anxiety. And all artists are at risk.

Rejection and Criticism

Rejection and criticism is part of an artist's life. It's a part that we would like to skip, but unfortunately that is not possible.

There will be one star reviews for this book, I can almost guarantee it. Does it make me sick? Absolutely. Does it make me want to stop writing it? Yes, sometimes, when I'm tired and I imagine all those negative readers who will pick apart every flaw and throw it back in my face. I imagine when I start giving workshops on the subject that people may heckle me because they don't like what they hear. I imagine the letters of rejection from agents when it is time to query my science fiction novel. And I remember the many times I've been rejected before and how it has impacted me.

In 2011, I applied to two film schools. At the time I didn't realise that the writing part was what interested me the most, but instead I wanted to learn how to direct. I had to prepare a short film project for one and a photography project for the other. It took me a lot of time to get everything ready and it was the first time since my depression that I

---

[6] Imposters have goals too: The imposter phenomenon and its relationship to achievement goal theory
Shamala Kumar, Carolyn M. Jagacinski
https://www.sciencedirect.com/science/article/pii/S0191886905002333?via%3Dihub
[7] Are all impostors created equal? Exploring gender differences in the impostor phenomenon-performance link
Rebecca L. Badawy, Brooke A. Gazdag, Jeffrey R. Bentley, Robyn L.Brouer
https://www.sciencedirect.com/science/article/pii/S0191886918302435

had attempted something so challenging.

I was rejected from both.

The pain was almost physical. This was the proof I was not good enough. This was the proof that all these dark feelings brought by my depression were right. I was not worth it. I was a failure.

Rejection at the wrong time can be disastrous for an artist. It can push you to never create. It can make you scared to try new things, or to put yourself in a situation where you could be rejected. I have seen performers who quit because they couldn't deal with auditions where they were rejected over and over. I have seen writers remove all their stories online because they got trolled by people who didn't like their work.

Yes, rejection is part of being an artist, but it doesn't mean that we know how to deal with it.

OTHER ISSUES

There are many other mental health issues and illnesses that are beyond the scope of this book. I think it is worth mentioning that one interesting study[8] examined the link between creativity and psychosis in historical figures and also recent patients, and concluded that mental illness was a hindrance to creative work, and not the source of it.

If you are interested in this subject, I suggest you read the book "Touched With Fire: Manic-depressive Illness and the Artistic Temperament" by Kay Redfield Jamison.

It is also beyond the scope of this book to discuss addictions, such as drugs and alcohol. If you are suffering from a disabling addiction, I

---

[8] Creativity and madness: New findings and old stereotypes.
Rothenberg, A. (1990). Baltimore, MD, US: Johns Hopkins University Press.
https://psycnet.apa.org/record/1990-98880-000

urge you to seek help with your nearest doctor. Addiction ruins lives, and artists are particularly vulnerable to using addictive substances or activities as coping mechanisms for the above issues.

A few resources to help you:

- The charity Mind in the UK keeps up to date resources to help you with addiction and dependency.
- The National Institute of Drug Abuse has a lot of information about different drugs and treatments in the US.
- The World Health Organisation offers statistics and documentations about substance abuse.

HELP YOURSELF

Re-program Your Thoughts

"Emotional first aid" is a concept that I was introduced to via another TED talk: "Why we all need to practice emotional first aid"[9] by Dr. Guy Winch. It explains how society is perfectly comfortable with healing the body, but unequipped to deal with problems of the mind. If you can spare fifteen minutes, I strongly advise you to watch it.

The idea is easy to understand and extremely difficult to apply: emotional first aid, or emotional hygiene, means checking the dialogue that you have with yourself. Are your thoughts making matters worse for you? If you suffer a rejection in your art, do you pile on it by saying to yourself that you deserved it, that you'll never be good enough, that you are not worth someone's attention?

Emotional first aid means reversing the years of bad habits that we have established with ourselves, the years of negative self-talk that make any situation ten times worse. If you receive criticism, you don't need to add to it with all you fears and doubts and negativity. Don't make the wound worse!

It is not an easy thing to do. When I was diagnosed with an anxiety disorder, I started the work with a therapist who immediately understood that anxiety was not my only problem. A major component

---

[9] Guy Winch, "Why we all need to practice emotional first aid" talk.
https://www.ted.com/talks/guy_winch_the_case_for_emotional_hygiene

of my anxiety was the way I was talking to myself all day long. Those thoughts were ranging from unhelpful to extremely destructive, depending on what was happening in my life. I used to have a commute to work that included a fifteen-minute walk. During this walk, it happened frequently that my mind got stuck on something minor, and transformed it into something big and ugly by the time I reached home. Winch calls it "ruminating". I would make myself so miserable that once or twice I arrived home with tears in my eyes. As you can see, I'm a champion at this.

I had to learn a different pattern for my thoughts. My therapist explained it this way:

> *"Our mind is like a pub, and the emotions and thoughts come and go. You can't prevent them from entering or leaving, but you can decide to let them influence you or not. Welcome them all, lead them to a table, give them a beer, but don't stay with them if you don't like them."*

It turns out rejecting a thought, fighting against it, makes it stronger. It always comes back, often with little friends, and torments you. Instead, you can say: "Thank you for sharing. Have a pint," and move on to a more constructive thought.

Constructive thoughts are the ones that help you heal emotional wounds. They are the ones that build your self-esteem instead of destroying it. They are the words that you would say to a friend, should they go through the same thing.

You can do this. It is a discipline — and guess what? — a habit. You can train yourself to do this. It might not solve everything, but it will provide you with the first line of defence against feeling miserable when you create.

You Don't Need to Suffer to Be Great

If there is a stereotype that I particularly dislike, it is the "tortured artist". It is the concept that you need to suffer to be a better artist, that there's only success in pain, and that if you are healthy and sane you will never be great.

What a load of rubbish.

Yes, some extremely talented artists were and are extremely tortured. The one example that comes to my mind is Kurt Cobain. I've been a fan of Nirvana since I was a teenager, and his suicide was a true shame. Did his demons and drug addiction make him a better musician? Perhaps in the short term, but it also robbed us of many more years of his creations.

This stereotype is dangerous because it can lead us to ignore mental health issues instead of trying to heal them. It can make us think that there is no other way, or fear that if we deal with our issues, we'll lose our creative spark. There's this idea that if you don't have any demons, you "don't have what it takes" to be successful.

If you have that stereotype in your mind, stop immediately! Plenty of successful creatives are not tortured. Of course, all of us pull inspiration from our experiences, good or bad, but it doesn't mean that it needs to kill us.

You don't need to torture yourself to be creative. Chances are, if you deal with your issues, you might find even more inspiration, or a different kind.

SURROUND YOURSELF WITH POSITIVE PEOPLE

Depending on the kind of artist you are, some of you can feel that nobody influences your art because you practice it alone. As a writer, I can sit in front of my computer and not interact with anyone all day long. But we are never truly alone in our lives, and I think it is important to observe the people around us.

Have you heard of the saying that you are the average of the five people you spend the most time with? While I think nowadays some of us can be close to more than five people, I agree with this. I think our close relationships influence us greatly.

Have you ever been having a drink with a friend and by the end felt exhausted and negative? On the other hand, have you ever been having a drink with another friend and felt rejuvenated, ready to take on any challenge? What is different? The friend, of course.

Some people will drag you down. It might seem obvious, but often we fail to recognise this in our closest relationships. How can you be a creative if you partner constantly denigrates your work? How can you decide to study art if your parents constantly pressure you to study science instead? How can you work towards making a living with your art if everyone around you tells you it is impossible?

The problem is, we don't always choose the people we spend time with. Have you ever had difficult colleagues? I once had a colleague tell me that my writing was a waste of time, that it was useless. Some acquaintances, plagued by their own insecurities, didn't take well to my pursuit of becoming a writer. I got plenty of criticism and sly remarks, designed to break me so they could feel better.

These are like poison. Every time someone's energy brings you down, it's more difficult to get up. You are not only battling your own problems, you are battling all their voices. And it's toxic.

What to do about it?

Depending on the type of relationship you have with the negative person, the approach will be different. Close family, friends, and partners need to be handled carefully. Is their negativity a passing feature, or have they always been like that? Is there a reason why they don't believe in you? Can you discuss it with them?

There is also a moment when you should establish **limits**. With a negative colleague, for example, this is when you can tell them that you don't want to engage in their bashing or gossiping. With toxic friends, instead of talking to them every day, you could reduce the time you see them. You can also request they don't talk about your art if they have nothing positive to say about it.

Then there's the most extreme solution of them all: you can stop associating with them altogether. This is something I have had to do over the years, and it is never easy. I tried everything else, but when a particular person made me feel so awful, lost, and overwhelmed, I had no choice. Sometimes, it is the only solution. Life is too short to let yourself get sucked dry by emotional vampires.

Removing toxic people from your social circle is only the first step. The second is much more joyful: surround yourself with people who will build you up; people who will make you feel valued and important; people who are naturally warm and creative. Sometimes it can be other artists, sometimes it can also be friends who are as excited as you are by your art.

It might seem that these kinds of people don't exist right now, or maybe they don't live where you live. I felt like that too when I went to university and only socialised with other scientists. That's when I discovered the internet, and the fanfiction community. That's why I'm still friends with some of the people I met there. For the first time in my life, it seemed, I was surrounded by people who had the same aspirations as me, even if it was in a virtual setting.

The more experienced you become with life and with your art, the more selective you'll be with your relationships. Don't allow negative people in your life. Like the meme says:

"Ain't nobody got time for that!"

STOP COMPARING YOURSELF TO OTHERS

Comparing yourself to other people, in particular other artists, is a natural process. It's human nature and, at least for some, can act as a booster for your art. When it becomes a problem, however, it is important to identify and stop unproductive ways of thinking.

How do we know that it is a problem? Here again, it is by observing your thoughts and noticing exactly what they are, that you'll be able to determine this. When you compare yourself to other artists, do you always come up short? Is every other creative person more productive, talented, successful, or popular than you? Do you use this comparison to push yourself down? Are you all criticism, never praise?

The problem is that society often encourages these comparisons, unaware of the devastating impact it has on creatives. When I spoke to a musical theatre performer about auditions in the West End, he told me stories of auditions where he entered a room and all the other men looked exactly like him. They all had the same general physique, and the same broad range of talents. They were put next to each other so that casting directors could compare and determine which one was the best for the role being cast that day. For performers in these conditions, it is impossible not to compare themselves to each other.

If your self-esteem is not at the right level, you come short. You perceive yourself as not good enough. It is sometimes even more cruel if you know these people, perhaps if you have trained with them. "Why them, and not me? Why am I always left on the side road? Why do I struggle while everything looks easy for them?"

If you are not careful, these thoughts can paralyse your creative process and open the door to all the issues we have discussed previously. So how do we fight this?

First of all, by forcing some objectivity into our thoughts. If you compared yourself to other people in an objective way, you would not get the short straw systematically. You would be less good than some people, true, but better than others. It's probability! And in reality, you would probably be better in some areas and worse in others. You would also not necessarily be able to compare, because someone's experience might be different to yours. How do you compare yourself to an artist who has a different way of comprehending the world? Of creating?

The second thing that helped me a lot was perfectly summarised during an interview:

> "We all have our time at different times." — Joseph O'Reilly, Performer

Some people see it as "fate", as a "plan", as "destiny". I'm not religious, but I am convinced that things happen for a reason, and that if I didn't get an opportunity, it was because something different was on the cards for me. Yes, it is frustrating when other people get something that I wanted, but maybe it is not what I needed. When I was rejected from the film schools I had applied to, I was extremely jealous of the people who had made it. I compared myself to them and I found myself clearly a loser. They were younger, more passionate, more talented and had better technical skills. I am now grateful that I was rejected. I would never have moved to London if I had got in, and I'm pretty sure I would not be writing this book right now.

Try to avoid triggers if you can. Social media is particularly cruel when it comes to comparisons. Everyone posts the best, edited version of themselves. They talk about their success, and rarely about their setbacks. It's easy to feel bad about yourself when you see all these high-achieving individuals in front of you. I am an avid Twitter user, but I've almost stopped using Facebook because it was making my "comparisonitis" worse. It was at a time when all my friends from high school were getting married, having babies, buying houses, getting promotions, while I was living in a garage-turned-studio, single and counting every penny. Facebook was too much of a trigger for me, so I eliminated it.

No matter what sets off your thoughts of comparison, make sure you notice them and challenge them. Make a habit of not accepting what your brain tells you at face value. Fact check it, see if it serves you. And if it's fake news, bin it!

Gratitude

I promise, this book is not about to turn into a mindfulness lesson. I have however tested a lot of methods over the years to make myself feel better and survive the life of a Part-Time Artist. One of them was gratitude. Gratitude means acknowledging the good things in our life and being thankful for them.

I had a hard time with it at the beginning. They don't teach you gratitude in school. They don't teach you to look behind and celebrate everything you have accomplished, the good things that have happened to you. If anything, I feel I've only been taught bitterness and resentment. So it was hard to switch gears and be happy with what I had, even if it appeared to be very little. To me, it sounded a bit too much like the "positive thinking" that people were talking about and that had never worked for me.

I think the difference between positive thinking and gratitude is that positive thinking feels artificial to me. How am I supposed to be positive at all times? Can I not feel sad sometimes? Do I need to put an immediate positive spin on everything, without acknowledging my true feelings? What if I can't? I think this can induce a lot of guilt and is not necessary helpful.

Gratitude, to me, looks much more sustainable. I am allowed to feel my feelings, no matter how dark they can become. These feelings fuel my writing too, so I don't necessarily want to get rid of all of them. But gratitude is there to remind me of the big picture, the fact that there is positivity even when everything gets dark.

It is also a way to stop myself spiralling down unnecessarily. When I have a particularly bad day, I get my gratitude journal from my bedside table and write down all the things I'm grateful for. It doesn't change the world, it doesn't change the situation that made me sad or angry in the first place, but it promotes another perspective in my mind, which is so prone to see everything as dark without nuance.

MEDITATION

Meditation is a practice that entails giving your attention to only one thing. It helps relaxing and calming your thoughts. There are many techniques of meditation, but the most basic one consists in breathing deeply for a few minutes.

I am not a specialist in meditation. I am not even good at it. At best, I can meditate maybe twenty minutes. Often I can't go past five minutes before becoming fidgety. Don't even get me started on trying to empty my mind. My mind is never empty.

I started meditating following the advice of my therapist, as a way to counter anxiety. I was far from thrilled at the idea, and felt defeated before I even started, which is probably why I haven't made much progress. However, I soon noted that even five minutes of meditation had a tremendous effect on my anxiety. Every time I do it, it is like a cool wave is invading my overheated mind and calms it down.

If you have never tried meditation and have the same reservations as me, I encourage you to take the leap. I can't meditate on my own, so I use YouTube videos. Having a voice that tells me what to concentrate on is helpful. Do it a few times, and see how you feel afterwards.

Many artists use meditation as a way to centre their creativity, and to relieve many stresses linked to it. Meditation can act as the start of a creative session, to put yourself in the right mindset, or it can be a way to cope with the many demands in your life.

Keep Track of the Good

If your mind is built the same way as mine, this is probably something you struggle with too. During my therapy, I was amazed that I was able to vividly recall some memories from when I was a child. But there was a catch: I could only remember the bad ones. The good ones seemed erased, or at least less vivid.

This is a subject that is studied by psychologists[10]. We tend to recall negative experiences much more clearly than positive ones. The current theory is that emotions enhance the process of memory retention, and that the part of our brain that deals with emotions "fuels" the part of our brain that deals with memory.

With this mechanism built into our brain, it means that over time the negativity can take a falsely disproportionate place in our mind. Again, I don't want to suppress negative thoughts entirely, but I think it is

---

[10] Remembering the Details: Effects of Emotion, Elizabeth A. Kensinger
https://www.researchgate.net/publication/24407465_Remembering_the_Details_Effects_of_Emotion

important to correct the bias that our brains naturally produce, because it doesn't objectively represent the truth of what has happened.

My way of doing that? I have a jar on my desk that is labelled "Achievements". Over the course of a year, I fill it with the achievements I have made. What do I consider an achievement? Anything — big or small — that made me proud to finish. It can be as huge as having a short story published in a magazine, or as little as making a dessert from scratch for the first time.

At the end of the year, when it is time to review my goals and set up my new ones for the next year, I get all the pieces of papers from the jar and I read them, one by one. Often, I have forgotten some of the achievements. It's crazy everything you do in a whole year, but if I hadn't kept track I might not have remembered some of it!

One of my interviewees had a great method of keeping track of the good things and remembering them: she has a book of quotes and advices. During her interview, Lauren Shields (singer) explained that after a long stint of unsuccessful auditions, she started this book that she now carries everywhere. In it, she writes down quotes, encouragement, and good advices given to her. It could be coming from various sources, and it could also come from people who helped her along the way, such as mentors or close friends. She opens the book often, when she needs to remind herself of some of its wisdom. It works for her.

I highly encourage finding a way to keep track of the good in your life, as it happens, for the benefit of your future self. Don't let your brain keep its bias towards negative experiences. Life is often composed of both positive and negative, and it's only fair to have a way to remember both.

Have a "Me" Day

Sometimes, it is worth being selfish. If you feel like you've spread yourself too thin, or haven't felt like yourself for a while, it is OK to take time to reset and re-centre yourself.

A "me" day can mean different things for different people. For me, a "me" day involves going somewhere other than London, armed with a notebook and my overwhelming feelings, to write down everything that comes to my mind. I also make sure I pamper myself a little, with maybe a massage or a great meal. I need this time to work out what bothers me or what makes me feel bad. Sometimes, it also means staying in bed all day and watching Netflix.

I need this from time to time to stay sane, and if you feel overworked, overwhelmed, or burned out, chances are you need it too.

I used to manage performers, and part of my job consisted of authorising their holidays. Most of my employees used to take holidays only to go and do a performing job or an audition. It was normal to never see them go on a real holiday, or to never use a real day off.

I did exactly the same when I was in their position. Days off work were too precious to waste on silly things like "resting" or "pampering". I can tell you exactly what this kind of schedule produces in the long term, after years of not having time for myself. Yes, you guessed it: burnout.

"Me" days should be treated as importantly as "creative" or "work" days. They should be planned the same way you plan the rest of your week, and it should be your first reflex when you start feeling overwhelmed.

Ask for Help

What I know from my personal experience is that if you face something that is stronger than you, that is preventing you from living your artistic life the way you want, you need to talk to someone about it. Friends, family or professionals. I will be 33 years old when this book comes out, and I have seen four different therapists in my life. All helped me in a way, all were priceless in my progress as an adult and as an artist.

I know asking for help will be difficult for a lot of you. It was difficult for me, too. Not many people know that I had therapy, and almost no one knows that I've seen four different professionals in my life. I am still ashamed, I guess, which is ridiculous. No one would make a fuss if I said I saw four different doctors for four different health problems. It is exactly the same for therapists.

Help can come from your friends or your family, if you decide to talk to them about your issues. It can come from your doctor. It can also come from strangers whose job it is to listen.

If you are struggling with something right now, I hope that this chapter might act as a trigger for you to get the help you need and deserve. You don't have to fight it alone, and you don't need all this crap in your art

Below, you'll find some helpful links and organisations:

- Mental Health hotlines per country: http://www.cocoonais.com/mental-health-hotlines-worldwide/
- Mental Health support per country: http://mentalhealth.wearespur.com/
- International Association for Suicide Prevention: https://www.iasp.info/
- The Samaritans, UK: https://www.samaritans.org/
- Lifeline, Australia: https://www.lifeline.org.au/
- Mental Health America, USA: http://www.mentalhealthamerica.net/
- It's OK To Talk, India: http://itsoktotalk.in/
- Africa Mental Health Foundation, Kenya: http://www.africamentalhealthfoundation.org/
- Telefono de la Esperanza, Europe and South America: http://www.telefonodelaesperanza.org/

Your Strategy

As I said at the beginning of this chapter, many artists will face mental health issues during their career. Perhaps you are facing one (or more) right now. Here are a few questions that might help you:

1) How does it feel for you? How does it impact you and your art? What does it prevent you from doing?

2) Have you tried to help yourself? How? Did it work? Did it fail?

3) Is there a strategy in this book that could help you? When do you plan on trying it? How?

Make a plan, like you would for every other part of your art career. Give yourself goals and reward yourself when you reach them. Use the companion book if it helps you to keep a track of your plan and of the strategies you think might help you.

And remember: you can ask for help!

CHAPTER SIX
DAY JOB & MONEY

THE JOB THAT WORKS WITH YOUR ART
THE JOB-TO-PAY-THE-BILLS

In this chapter, I am going to talk about the other activity that is most of the time necessary for us artists: the day job. I will offer you my point of view not only as an artist myself with twelve years balancing between jobs and writing, but also as an ex-manager who used to hire artists and work with them on a daily basis.

This chapter is designed to help you no matter what stage in your career you are. You could have graduated and be looking for a job, be in the same job for years, looking to change, or frankly hating anything that is not your art. I hope you'll find useful advice no matter what your situation is.

WHAT KIND OF JOB?

Broadly speaking, there are two types of day jobs that artists will have: the temporary, often low-skilled job to earn money until art can pay the bills, and the long-term, committed career. Depending on your goals as an artist, you will go for one or the other.

Out of curiosity, I recently asked on Twitter what kind of jobs the creatives I was following had, and I got a myriad of different replies: teaching, healthcare, administrative work, customer service, IT, archaeology, legal, charity... I was amazed at how diverse artists' other careers are. Generally, artists with a long-term career fared better in terms of feeling good about what they did on a daily basis than those with temporary jobs, but of course there were exceptions.

You should give a lot of thought about what you want to do and why. A bad day job can be devastating for your artistic career. You will spend a lot of time at work, even if you are only part-time, and if you are unhappy during these long hours, it is going to bleed out into the rest of your life.

Think about organisation first. How is your job going to work with your obligations as an artist? For example, a lot of actors and performers need flexibility to be able to go to auditions. They'll tend to converge towards hospitality jobs that can offer them flexible shifts. Some artists might prefer having the possibility of normal weekends where they can make their art, therefore they'll search for a "nine to five". Some might be parents, which brings another layer of complication, because the job needs to work with your art and with your schedule as a parent.

Then think about your skills and what you are good at. I am an extrovert who can talk to anyone without feeling stressed about it. This is why I ended up in customer service, because it was something that I could do pretty easily. I also liked meeting a lot of people, even despite the fact that some of them were rude or demanding. What are your skills? What kind of industry would fit you best? You also need to take in account how likely you are to find a job in this particular industry, and if you need a specific training or degree to do them.

Think about your goals. Do you want to stay in this type of jobs for the rest of your career, while doing art on the side? Or do you want a job that you can quit easily when you get an artistic opportunity? If a job gets in the way of your art career, you are more likely to resent it and to be unhappy there.

Finally, think about the atmosphere. Do you want to be surrounded by other artists? Do you want to work alone? Would you rather be in a large corporation or work in a smaller business? While you can't predict how good your colleagues and your bosses will be, you can already decide what kind of structure will work best for you.

You will spend a lot of time at work, whether you like it or not. So it is worth spending a little time making sure you get the right one, instead of rushing and choosing the first job you see.

Finding a Job

As a manager, I used to see a lot of CVs from all kinds of artists, but mostly from performers, and I was shocked at how bad most of them were. Writing a CV and a cover letter are not difficult skills to learn, but they are often forgotten by dramatic or artistic schools. Most people I spoke to have never been taught how to write a CV properly, and especially not for a day job.

One important rule to remember is that you need a different CV for your art and for your day job. I used to receive so many "performer" CVs that were obviously not adapted for non-creative job hunting. It looked unprofessional and lazy. It is important that you adapt your CV to whoever you are applying to. A potential employer is not going to care about your film credits or your painting exhibitions, for example. You can always list them under another section, for example "artistic projects" to show your passion, but it shouldn't be the principal attraction of your CV. Quite honestly, most employers don't care about your art.

Think about what an employer wants from you. They want to know the answer to four major questions:

1) Do you have the skills to do the job?
2) Do you have experience in the same industry?
3) Are you going to be easy to work with?
4) Will you be committed to the company?

Your CV should reply to these questions within one page or at maximum two. List the skills that you have that are relevant to the job. List your relevant experiences (you don't have to list all of them, just the most important ones). Always start with the most recent, unless it is customary to do otherwise. If you don't have professional experience, list projects you have participated in that gave you the relevant skills. Be honest! And stay positive about all these experiences, which will show that you are easygoing. If an employer thinks you might be a diva, they won't invite you to an interview.

A cover letter should also be personalised to each job. When I was looking for a job, I used a template that I modified each time to suit the company to which I was applying. Research them for a little while. It doesn't have to take long. Once you have a system, every letter should not take more than half an hour.

During the interview, concentrate on the same questions. Talk about your skills, your experience and stay positive. Show your willingness to work for them. Don't talk about your art unless they ask you about it. Again, most employers don't care! Worse, it could be a deterrent if they think you won't take the job seriously.

How to Survive the Job

There are two types of attitude you can adopt when facing your day job: you can make the best of it, or you can make the worst of it.

I often see artists who get a job, and do the bare minimum because it is not their dream career. They bring nothing to the table and make themselves miserable in the process. They are in the constant mindset of, "I hate this, I'll soon be out". Except that most of the time, it takes much longer than they would like to get out of there.

On the other hand, I see fantastic employees who are aware that their job is not their dream, but who have decided that, since they are there, they'll do the best they can. These people have decided to make the best of a non-ideal situation.

I strongly believe that there's a silver lining to most jobs, even if you don't appreciate it at the time. A few years ago, I was fired from a job because of a dispute over remuneration. It was a dreadful experience all around, and I still feel angry about it. However, recently, I had to use a skill that I learned there. I hadn't used it since the job, but because I knew it, it made my life easier. That job, while in the top five of the worst jobs I've ever had, allowed me to do something today that I wouldn't have otherwise been able to.

In my experience, those who have a positive outlook on their day jobs are also the ones who manage to fit more creative time around it. They waste less energy hating what they do every day and concentrate on what it brings them instead.

Leaving Work at Work

There is something that a lot of artists have issues with: prioritising their art, not with their time, but with their mind. It means not letting problems, stress, or anxiety linked to your job pollute your creativity.

I was not good at this. I had a hard time compartmentalising the different aspects of my life. When I'm stressed because of work, my writing gets crappy. When I'm upset about something else, it tends to paralyse my writing. Hell, when I'm mad at someone, I am likely to write them being atrociously murdered in my next story!

I have had to learn over the years to leave work at work.

There are certain things that can help you make a transition in your brain, to make yourself understand that "job time" is over, and that it's "art time" or "family time" now. I have a ritual that I did every day when I came home from work. I changed immediately and removed make-up and jewellery. Changing clothes triggered a different mindset in my brain, saying that no matter what had happened earlier that day, it was over now.

Venting also helps, no matter how petty it sounds. I did vent to my partner when I got home, because it's important to not keep bad experiences inside. If you don't, it may keep tormenting you long after you came home and ruin the rest of your day. If you don't have someone to vent to, journaling is a good alternative. I have years of journals full of rants in my desk!

When I've had a particularly bad day, I also turn to meditation. As explained before, I am not good at it, but it can help quiet my overactive mind. Even a short period, ten minutes, can prevent a ruined evening.

Another strategy you can use to leave work at work is to make work less stressful. As I covered in the chapter about energy, you don't need to give a hundred percent every day, every hour. The more you learn to let go, take breaks, and enjoy yourself, the easier it will be at the end of the day to leave it all behind.

The trick is to make sure that you have reminders of your real goals, of your real passion, for when you feel overwhelmed, and to know that these goals don't prevent you from doing a good job. Taking breaks, as long as they are reasonable, makes you a better and more focused employee, and a better artist after work.

Observe your behaviour at work and outside. How many times does work cross your mind when you're at home? Does it constantly stay in your thoughts? Can you take a break to re-centre yourself?

When to Quit

There are jobs, however, that are not worth the trouble. When there's absolutely nothing redeemable about the work, the environment or the employer, that's when it's time to change.

I understand that some jobs are terrible, that some employers treat you like dirt, and that you would rather do your art all day long than work for them. I get it! When I was working in science, and being psychologically abused by my boss, I used to wish I would get into an accident. Not a bad one, but just enough so I would be unable to work for a while and I could stay home. When it reaches that point, it is important to decide to quit, because it will probably never get better.

Remember what is the most important: your art. A job is a mean to an end, a way to earn money, to meet people, to make life experiences perhaps. But it is JUST. A. JOB. Not your whole life. Not your self-worth. Not your art. If your job gets in the way of doing your best art, if it makes you miserable to the point where you can't create anymore, it is not worth it.

However, quitting a day job should be thought about seriously and you should have a fall-back plan. I suggest researching and making sure you know what you want. Do you want to stay in the same industry, but don't like the actual job? Perhaps re-training is needed before you can branch out. Do you like the job itself but hate the company? Don't be afraid to apply to competitors. Finally, do you want to change industry? Depending on what it is, you might have to start at the bottom of the ladder and climb up again.

Always remember what is the most important for you — your "why". Bringing money home is important, but not at the cost of your art, your happiness, and your family.

Your Day Job

Honestly assess your activities. Do they work with your art? Do they leave you enough time or energy to work on your projects? Do you feel miserable or is there a silver lining?

If you plan on finding a job or changing job, do you have all the tools you need? Is it the right time? Do you have a plan?

Are you able to draw a line between your work time and your art time? If not, why not? What could you change to achieve separation?

Do you have plans to progress in your job? How will that work in a few years?

Fill these up carefully, take time to do so. With this thinking, you might have to make difficult decisions, which is why it is important to take your time. Ask for advice from around you or from other artists. Get as much help as you can and move bravely towards your best life!

MAKING MONEY

STARVING ARTIST?

Sometimes it feels like money is the biggest problem for artists. The stereotype is that an artistic mind is not made for budgeting, dealing with taxes, or multiplying streams of income. Whether it's true or not, there's the enduring cliché of the starving artist. Worse, most non-artistic people don't even know that there's money to be made in art, which is paradoxical when you know that some works of art, such as the Harry Potter franchise, bring billions to their rights holders (and not only to J. K. Rowling herself).

Having a day job alleviates the anxiety linked to not having money, and that's why I think it is a good arrangement. But if your goal is to one day go full time with your art, or to at least reduce your work hours, there are a few concepts which I think are important to talk about.

BUDGETING

Probably the hardest step is the process of getting your finances together, and it is also the most important one. If you are an adult, you need to learn how to budget. There is nothing worse than having a ton of debt when trying to make it as an artist. You want savings and you want a safety net.

Even if your goal is not to become a full-time artist, you should have a budget, if only to have peace of mind when it comes to money. Think of it this way: you are spending a lot of energy at work to earn this money. Do you want to waste more energy on worrying about the fact that this money always seems to disappear before the end of the month? You could use this energy on your art instead.

In this section I will not preach something I haven't done myself. I know that some of you might be starting with disadvantages such as huge student debts or no support from your family, but it doesn't mean that you can't benefit from writing a budget.

The first thing I did, when I was living on minimum wage, was to write down all my spendings. It is tedious, but it is necessary if you want to know what you spend your money on. I love spreadsheets, so I've made one to help me streamline the process. I've uploaded a copy on the website for you to use:

www.theparttimeartist.com/helpful-tools

Every month, I write down everything I spend, and I divide the spendings into categories: food, transport, bills, etc. That's the first step. Observing your spending during a couple of months can help you identify trends and any unnecessary spendings.

The next step is to add what you should in theory spend in these categories. Your "target". This is important, because it will help you moderate yourself, especially if you tend to avoid looking at your bank account when you are ready to spend on something you know you don't need. Be mindful of why you overspend. Is it a coping mechanism, is it linked to how you feel or to what happened that month?

Next, I write how much I earn, so that I can calculate the difference between what I have earned and what I have spent:

What I Have Earned - What I Have Spent = Money Pot

If the money pot is zero or negative, you need to observe each category and see which ones went above target. What can you reduce? What is necessary? Don't try to lower everything at once, go gradually. Be mindful of the "money stealers", the little spending that, accumulated, destroys your budget. You might need to test this for a few months before you manage to achieve your targets in each category. Your goal at this stage is to end the month with something in the money pot.

Now, what do you do with your money pot? That's when things get interesting! I divide it into different, smaller pots, inspired by the JARS system developed by T. Harv Eker[11].

I divide my pot in five categories:

- **Savings**: One important thing to have is a "rainy day" fund. Money that sits there until you REALLY need it. Medical bills, car breaking down, you name it. This fund for emergencies is the first you should fill, and you should have a target for it. I keep six months of spending in there, just in case. It has no other purpose than making sure I don't become homeless because of one instance of bad luck.
- **Luxury**: This is almost as important as the savings. I've been budgeting my life for five years, and the reason it worked is because I treated myself for time to time. Saving is good, but if you are going to break down after six months, it's not going to work. Keep a little bit of money to have fun!
- **Writing Career**: This is the money that I save for opportunities that will arise in my artistic career. For example, this is the fund that helps me pay for my editor, or for a cover artist. This money pays for conventions and workshops. For me, this is the proof that I take my artistic career seriously: I put money into it.
- **Charity**: I am a big believer in helping others, and every month I give money to charities. Giving back a little is good for the world. It is also a mental exercise recommended by T. Harv Eker, to counteract a scarcity mindset. The idea is that money is abundant and that you can spare some for other people who need it. If you have never done it, consider contributing.
- **Financial Freedom**: This is the money that I invest and/or

---

[11] The JARS system, by T. Harv Eker.
https://blog.harveker.com/6-step-money-managing-system/

save for an investment in the future. This money is to help with my retirement, with buying a property, with doing all the things that I used to think were inaccessible to an artist like me.

You can add or remove categories from the budgeting spreadsheet, as you wish, and you can change the percentage associated with them to reflect how you want to work with your money. The most important thing is to do it, and to have goals with the money you have left.

What if there isn't much in the money pot?

If it gives you any hope, the first month I started this system I had £5 left at the end of the month. Five £1 coins. So I used five mugs, labelled them with my five categories, and put one coin in each mug. It wasn't much, and frankly I felt a little pathetic with my almost empty mugs. I could have spent these £5 on something. But the next month, with almost no further effort on my part, I had £10 left instead of £5.

After several changes of jobs, and raises, I don't use the mugs anymore. The amounts involved are much bigger, so I've replaced them with bank accounts. But the idea stays the same. Doing this kind of work, no matter how boring it is, helped me focus on growing money instead of burying my head in the sand and spending money quicker than I earned.

Worries about Money

If I'm so preachy about budgeting, it is because I know exactly what it feels like to have no money at all. To have your card declined because you were waiting for a cheque that hasn't cleared yet. To worry about the interest rate on your credit card and if you'll be able to repay it.

Worries about money are horrible, and it was the most powerful reason why I made sure I had a steady, well-paying job alongside my writing.

Before I did this, I was constantly worrying. I had a string of short-term low-paying jobs, and I was not writing much because I was too busy trying to find ways to stay afloat. I accepted any kinds of job, even ones that I hated, because I needed money. I did a customer service job in a company that treated its employees so badly that I seriously considered quitting after three days. But I didn't, because I couldn't. I needed the money too badly. I worked awfully long hours, double shifts, sometimes in the cold without heating. All of that because I couldn't afford not to. And all this time, I barely wrote.

I became so fed up of being poor. It seemed like all my friends were making tons of money, buying cars and houses, while I couldn't even afford a coffee. It was a low point in my life.

I decided that I couldn't let these worries prevent me from writing. I worked on getting better paying jobs, climbing the ladder, saving as much as I could. I never want to be in that position ever again. It was too soul crushing. I worked hard to get myself out of debt, and into a much more stable position.

And guess what? I've never written as much as I did after making that decision!

Is Money the Root of Evil?

I wonder why, as artists, we seem to have such a bad rapport with money. Before I started budgeting, I was almost rejecting everything that had anything to do with money. Money felt dirty. I was not an artist for money. Money was vile. Money was the opposite of what I wanted to do with my books. For me, money made everything evil.

I realised that it was what I had always been taught, from a young age. Of course, there are things that are much more important than money, but it had always been talked about in a negative way. I had been told that people who have a lot of money are necessarily bad people; told that art is pure, and pure is not compatible with money; told that freedom is more important for an artist than money.

That last one is funny when I think about it now. I quit my job in science to be free. To be the person I'm supposed to be. However, when I was struggling with money, I was not free. I was the opposite of free. Yes, I didn't have many strings attaching me anywhere, but I couldn't quit a job I hated because I needed to pay my bills. That wasn't freedom. That was foolishness.

Do you have a bad relationship with money too? Where does it come from? Is it justified? Does it prevent you from progressing and making enough money to survive?

A bad relationship with money is the first reason why artists don't dare to market themselves. It's like putting prices on our creations or on ourselves is taboo. If this is the case for you, bear with me.

Spending Money on Your Art

Art can be expensive to pursue. Whether it is classes, workshops, materials, or paying for freelancers to help you, the costs can run very high.

I think it is possible to make art on a budget. You don't need to spend a fortune to do what you are passionate about. The idea is to be smart about it. First, ask yourself if you can do it for free or for very little money. There are tons of options out there to get results for free. Whether it's open source softwares, salvaging materials, using schools or public facilities, there are many ways to get what you need without spending a penny.

Learning to do some things yourself can also save you a lot of money. For example, you can learn to do your own website. It's not as complicated as it seems! Or you can ask for help from your friends or family. My aunt, Aline Mhote, designed my personal website. It was fun to work with her, and afterwards she used my website to publicise her design business.

Talking about exchange of services, this is also a way you could get something for much less. There are freelancers and artists who need to build a portfolio and would be happy to work with you as long as you give them a testimonial. It's a win-win situation.

Crowdfunding is another way of financing a project that might not have been possible otherwise. I made my first short film in London, Sherlock Holmes and the Stolen Emerald, thanks to a crowdfunding in 2012. I would never have been able to pay for it without the generosity of the people who backed the project.

Finally, having a fund for your art is important. As you have seen in the budgeting section, I have a "writing fund", which means that I save money every month for opportunities that might come. It helps me know how much I can spend and sieve through the options more easily.

However you choose to spend money on your art, make sure you don't put yourself in a bad situation because of it. Don't take loans or go into debt because of a project, unless you are 100% sure that you will get your money back somehow. The stress that it would generate is not worth it.

> *"There is a preconceived idea that you need to spend to accumulate. It's something that people say all the time. In a very logical way it works, but it can be dangerous. You need to assess the return you get from what you spend. I've spent tens of thousands of pounds in training and lessons, but more recently I've tried to invest in things that genuinely will help me."* — Lauren Shields, Singer

MAKING MONEY FROM YOUR ART

In this section, I'm going to talk about making money, yes, but not necessarily enough money to survive. The idea here is to change your mindset about what can be done to earn a little bit of money from your art. Think of it as another stream of income, aside from your job. In the next chapter, I'll talk about how to turn this into a full-time income, if your plan is to go full-time one day.

So, getting some money from your art. Seems impossible? It did to me, too, for the longest time.

Depending on the type of artist you are, the ways to achieve this can be different. Performers are not going to earn the same way as painters, for example. For some of you, it is all about selling a product. For many, it is about selling yourself.

A concept that kept coming back in my interviews with artists for this book was: know your worth. In other words, don't sell yourself cheap. It is common for all artists, and unfortunately it is pushed on us by society and some artistic communities.

Let's say you are a musician and you are looking for gig opportunities. More often than not, you'll have people offering you these opportunities with a catch: it's for "exposure only". This is where problems start. While it is perfectly understandable to do exposure only gigs when you start your career, it comes a point where you have to put a price on your talents. And usually, artists are pretty bad at making this transition.

I am exactly the same. I wrote fanfiction for twelve years, and of course didn't get any money from it. I transitioned into writing short stories, scripts, and more recently a novel. All still unpaid. I thought, "I'm not good enough to ask for money. I need to learn more. These are good opportunities." And while these reasons are perfectly valid, they were also a way to delay the "big leap", because I was afraid.

What if I get paid and they don't like what I produce? What if I'm not good enough? What if I don't finish the project? When you enter money into the equation, it immediately adds a lot of pressure to perform, and it starts feeling less like art and more like a chore.

The trick is to go for it gradually and to try new things. A few months ago, I received a paid opportunity for a short film script. I felt afraid but excited about the project. I had a good feeling about the story and about the person who had contacted me to write it. So I took the leap and I did it. It was the first time in my life that I had been paid for my writing. It was not a lot of money by any standard, but it was enough to change something in the way I think about my art. For the first time, my brain believed in my potential.

Now, I am redesigning all my projects to make some money out of them. This book is the first I have written with the purpose of making a living out of it. I use things like affiliate marketing to make my blog profitable. I plan on conducting workshops and other projects in extension to this one. Does it mean that I'm suddenly evil and that I'm only in this for the money? Absolutely not. I enjoy writing this book and I do it without knowing if it will make any money. I have immensely enjoyed interviewing artists and hearing what they needed and what they wanted. I can't wait to meet more of you during my workshops. It's a passion project before anything else, but I want it to make some money so I can do more!

Can you make some money out of your art? It doesn't need to be a lot, just a starting point. Can you sell something? Or appear in a paid gig? Select one thing that you can do for money. Ideally, it shouldn't take a lot of time to do, and should not distract you from your bigger projects. Can you allocate one hour a week to it, perhaps? Or a whole session? Make it a priority for a little while, and push it to the end. Make sure you are not stopping until you see the money, even if the money doesn't cover your costs.

Assess what it feels like to get money for your creation. Did you enjoy the process? Do you want to repeat it? Or did the project drag along? Do you want to try with something different? Or is it not for you?

TAXES

No chapter on money for artists would be complete without a note on taxes. Taxes are the most boring, annoying, achingly disagreeable subject I can imagine talking about in a book. It is, however, unavoidable. If you start earning money from your art, you will have to worry about taxes.

I have lived in three different countries with three different sets of tax rules, so my goal here is not to explain them in details. That would be pointless if it is not specific to your situation. However, I urge you to research the subject yourself instead of avoiding it.

Much like budgeting, taxes are something we tend to push back far away from our thoughts until we have to concentrate on it, usually when there's a deadline we can't avoid. By that point, it has turned into such a huge mountain that it is forever marked as "impossible" in our mind.

I think there's a better way to do this, the same as budgeting: write down your expenses and revenues as they come, and keep a record. I have made a simple monthly business accounting spreadsheet that you can download from the website:

www.theparttimeartist.com/helpful-tools

That's the one I am using, as my business is straightforward. Every month, I print the corresponding sheet and file it along with receipts, invoices and other proofs needed. Once I reach the end of the year, I can easily work out my expenses and my revenues, and complete my tax return. Don't forget that some items that you use for your creative process might be tax deductible. For example, for writers, books (including fiction) count as personal development and are therefore tax deductible. It is the same for anything that can be classed under research or personal development.

You can also use an online software or an app to help you in this work. It can also help you generate invoices and track payments, if your business requires it. For example, my editor Vicky Brewster uses Quickbooks to make her life easier.

Once again: ignoring your tax responsibilities will not make them go away. If you spend a little bit of time each month, it will be an easier task than cramming all of the work near the deadline.

CHAPTER SEVEN
GOING FULL-TIME

PROS AND CONS

MY EXPERIENCE

Recently, I have become a full-time writer, after twelve years of doing it on the side of a day job. I didn't make this decision lightly, and it took me a year to go from the abstract thinking to the concrete action of quitting my job, in January 2019.

Twitter:
@CelineTerranova - 5:49 PM - 14 Jan 2019
Today is my birthday. Today, I have also resigned from a job that made me depressed, to concentrate on taking my writing business to the next level. This project is really really exciting! So YAY for being 33, unemployed and happy!

During this time, I weighed pros and cons, I considered what kind of business I wanted and how I was going to go about it, and I saved money for the big leap.

I quit my job before my business was fully launched because I knew I could afford living a couple of months without a salary, and because my job had become unbearable for unrelated reasons. I don't know yet if this gamble will pay off so I have a plan B, in case it doesn't work.

If you are thinking about going full-time, this chapter is there to help you in the beginning of the process. I lay out all the important steps that helped me make a decision and organise the business. I hope this will help you too!

STABILITY VS FREEDOM

I have had a day job since I was 21. I've also had a couple of unemployed months, and these were stressful times in my life. Having a job is reassuring and is exactly the reason why we are Part-Time Artists in the first place. Becoming freelance or a company owner means that you lose this safety, this stability. Money can come and go, and you might never know when the next pay check is going to come.

This can be stressful — it is stressing me out too!

On the other hand, being a full-time artist means that you can have much more freedom. Depending on what you do, you might not even need to be attached to one place. You could travel and create at the same time, and that's a kind of freedom you'd struggle to get with a regular job. You would not need to take a day off to go to a doctor's appointment, for example. You would not need to count your holiday days to make sure you can go to a relative's wedding. Or you can decide to have a day off when you are exhausted.

But again, maybe you won't be able to afford to take a day off, even if you are sick. Or go on holiday. Or go to the doctor.

This is a mental ping pong that you might have played out in your head before, and these are important considerations to think about before you make any decision. What do you value the most?

It doesn't mean that you can't be stable with a freelance job or free with a day job, but I believe it is important to know what to expect when you make a decision about going full-time.

Do What You Love...

... and you'll never work a day? I've heard this countless of times, but I am a realistic person and I don't believe it is entirely true. In every job, passion or not, there are parts of it that are annoying. You will have to run every aspect of your business, no matter if you like it or not.

For example, as a writer, I also have to be able to do marketing, accounting, web design, customer service and sales. A lot of artists don't want to have to deal with all of these side activities that are necessary to any business.

If you are thinking about going full-time, make sure you don't idealise the work and the life that you will have. Talk to other artists who do what you want to do. Ask questions about their day-to-day activities, and ask them what parts of their job they don't like doing, or the obstacles they have had to overcome. Being informed is the best way to prepare yourself for what is to come. If you think that the life of a full-time artist is rainbows and daisies, you're in for a cruel wake-up call. Even famous artists have to do boring stuff sometimes.

Make sure you also ask about the benefits lacking in a freelance job.

Depending on your country, you might not have access to unemployment pay, maternity/paternity leave, pension, or healthcare. This is also part of the life of a full-time artist, and it is something you should know before you make a decision. Further than a question of money, these benefits make a steady job more attractive than the simple question of salary.

Who Do You Want to Be?

Something that helped me deciding if I wanted to go full-time was imagining what kind of person I wanted to become. I used to project myself five or ten years in the future and imagine what my life could be. If I projected myself as progressing in my day job, it didn't make me excited at all. However, when I imagined being a businesswoman, with my art being at the forefront of my life, it was giving me butterflies in the stomach.

I had no idea how I would make it, of course, but this exercise of visualisation helped me develop my intuition for things that I wanted and things that I didn't want, and it shaped my path up until today.

Take a few minutes and project yourself into the future. Imagine different scenarios and check how you feel about them. Do you see yourself rocking the day job and enjoying a good balance with your art? Or do you feel better imagining yourself as a self-employed person? Do you imagine having a team working under you?

You can even go further and imagine how you would tell the story of your life to your grand-children or to an biographer. What would make you proud? What adventures happened to you?

This work should give you a good insight into what you want.

YOUR ARTISTIC BUSINESS

YOUR BUSINESS PLAN

If you have decided that you want to pursue your art full-time, first of all congratulations! It is a bold move, and you should be proud of yourself. But now, it's time to design a strategy.

A business plan is something that can seem daunting at first, but it is the first step of any lasting business. I lay out the steps in the following sections in a way that, I hope, will make it easy to understand and apply to your circumstances.

You can use the workbook to fill up your answers and keep a track of your thoughts. You can always modify it later when you refine your ideas.

WHY?

We always come back to the same question: why do you want to do your art? Why do you feel like you should do it full-time? There will be a lot of hurdles on the way to making a full living with your art, so your "why" needs to be powerful and meaningful.

It cannot be just because you hate your job. It cannot be just because you want some free time. It cannot be just because you want to be famous. While these reasons can be there, I don't think they are strong enough to get you through all the bad times.

I have wanted to run my own business for almost ten years. I made several attempts before, with projects that had nothing to do with writing, but they failed because I was not passionate enough to continue through the obstacles. So you not only need a "why", you also need a "why this". Why this in particular? Why is this the thing you are prepared to do until you make it? Why is this the thing you will introduce yourself as when you meet new people? Why is this the thing that will work?

I think my previous ventures also failed because I was not ready. I was in debt, I was not fully ready to perform in English, and I didn't have the contacts I needed. You also need a "why now". Why is this the right time for this business? Why is it the right time in your particular sector? Why is it the right time in your life?

Take some time, and next to your "why", write your "why this" and "why now". Be specific. This is the base of your work, and it will help you immensely when things get tough.

What?

Now that you have your strong reasons to start, let's have a look at what you are going to do exactly.

If you are lucky, you can earn money by doing exactly what you love to do. For example you can be a painter, work on the paintings that inspire you and sell them. This is, however, rare, especially if you are at the beginning of your career. I write science fiction books and, even if I get an agent and get published, I won't probably make enough to pay my bills. You might already know that it doesn't matter how talented you are, if most people don't get paid for it, you probably won't either.

The good news is, there's another way! Most full-time artists I know can afford to be full-time because the centre of their money-making business is **something related to their art that is proven to make money**.

Here are a few examples:

- Teach classes on your subject
- Work on commercials for actors or filmmakers
- Be an extra in a shoot
- Use the power of social media and have an Instagram related to your art that is sponsored
- Have a monetised YouTube channel or podcast related to your art
- Write a blog related to your art with affiliate links
- Sell or licence your artwork to be used on websites
- Write a book about it
- Find a way to make your bestselling pieces quicker and market them exclusively
- Use service websites like Fiverr or Upwork to market your talents
- Host conferences or workshops where you can invite fellow artists.

Think about what makes money in your art. Follow other artists and see what they do. Don't limit yourself to one money-making avenue. Quite the opposite: you will need several streams of income, in case one of them dries out.

My plan for my own business is exactly that. The Part-Time Artist is just the beginning. I fully intend on marketing this book to my social media following, and reach a good selling level on Amazon and other platforms, but this won't be my only way of making money. I will organise workshops and coaching sessions on the same subject, where I can help other artists in a more direct way. These will bring money too, and allow me to sell physical copies of the book at the same time. I have a blog where I recommend products that helped me and that I think will help my target audience. I am planning on starting either a YouTube channel or a podcast, and I am already planning the sequel to The Part-Time Artist.

As you can see, I don't put all my eggs in the same basket. I am also doing something slightly different from my initial passion of writing science fiction, but that is related enough that I love what I'm doing. The Part-Time Artist venture will replace my day job, and I will keep writing fiction on the side.

Make a list of everything that you could do to make money related to your art. Make sure you spend time on this, and be specific. It doesn't matter if it is not currently feasible. Just make sure you have them on paper.

Who?

When you talk about making money, you need to think about who is going to give you that money. In other words, who are your customers? What makes them good candidates to buy what you are selling?

Let's say you are a performer and you are planning to put a show on the road and find venues across the country. Who will be the audience? What will be the venues that will book you? Why them? What makes them more likely to part with their money for what you are offering?

A lot of people in the business world talk about "target audience". The thing is, your creations won't appeal to everyone, and it would be a big waste of energy to try to. Instead, you should concentrate on a section of the public that you know is already interested.

What is your target demographic? Sometimes it is defined by an age category. Sometimes it is defined by a gender. Sometimes it is defined by cultural interests. Whatever you use, be specific. You should have a crystal clear image of the people you are addressing, as it will make your marketing much more targeted and therefore more efficient.

By "who" I also mean: "Who are you?" It is as important as your customer. What are your talents, skills, experiences that make you the unique person that your customers are going to buy from. Why are you the best person for this job? Why should they trust you?

Most people part with their money only if they trust that they have made a good decision. Which means that you will have to prove it to them! Write it down, the same way you would write an "about me" section on your website. Make sure you point out all the things that make you the right person for this job, product, or service. It has nothing to do with bragging, but reminding yourself and your customers that you are a trustworthy source of the thing they want to pay for.

When?

Now that you have your product or service, and your target audience, it is time to plan your schedule.

A lot of businesses fail before even starting because they have no real timely goals. The same way you wrote your goals as a Part-Time Artist, you need to do the same as a full-time one. When are you going to launch your product? How many months before you are ready? What do you need to do in the meantime? What is your deadline? What will you do after the launch?

Giving yourself deadlines is a major component of your art business. If you write a book and want to launch it, you have to give yourself a target by which you should be ready.

Deadlines are scary, and often artists go about them the wrong way. When we talked about goals earlier, we talked about making them S.M.A.R.T. One of the components of this acronym was "achievable". Your goals should not depend on someone else's input, and your deadlines shouldn't either.

Let's say that you are waiting for a venue to get back to you. Your goal cannot be "the venue will get back to me by the end of February", because you have no control on that. Instead, try "If the venue doesn't get back to me by the beginning of the month, I'll contact them again, and three other venues to be safe."

It is also important to take in account big steps in your schedule. When do you plan to quit your job? When do you plan to go public with your idea? And don't forget to take into account obstacles that will impair your productivity. For example, if you have a busy schedule around Christmas, don't plan on editing a whole book like I did!

Be specific on your deadlines for the next year at least, and make sure you update your schedule as things go. The schedule is most probably going to change along the way. This is normal, and you should concentrate on being flexible and responsive to your market. Keep going, correct the course, and keep an eye on your deadlines.

How?

The last part of your art business is money. After all, you are trying to make a living with your art, so it is important to set yourself clear goals in terms of finances.

How are you going to receive money? It might seem straightforward, but if your business is mainly online, you might run into several hurdles. For example, I had an issue with the payment to my illustrator, Juan Carlos Porcel. As he lives in Bolivia, I couldn't use something like Paypal because it didn't allow money to be received in that country. We had to find another solution, and it was a headache. Make sure your customers don't have to jump through too many hoops to pay you, otherwise you risk losing them. Have a foolproof plan to get paid, with minimum fees if possible.

Another important question to ask yourself is "How much?" How much you need, exactly. You currently probably have a salary — do you need all of it? Will you need your current level of spending once you go freelance? Will you need more, to compensate for the loss of a pension or healthcare? Or will you need less, due to your change of standards of living or reduced commuting costs?

Have a look at your budget and sort what you need and what you don't. For example, I used to have a big expense in travelling, as my travel card for the tube in London was expensive. I used to go to Central London every day, so I didn't have a choice. When I became freelance and travelled less, this big expense was reduced. I know some artists who have moved to a different city or to a smaller house. You have to take these things into account to realistically answer the above question.

Write it down: how much money do you need per month and per year? Don't forget that this is the net amount of what you need. At the beginning, you might not make enough money to pay taxes, but if your business thrives you will need to add at least 20% to account for the taxes. Add also the savings you still intend to make, and the benefits you used to have.

Once you have this number, the next step is to calculate how you will earn it. How much will you value your product or service? And how many of them will you have to sell to reach your goal? What are your other streams of income and how much will they bring to you? It is important to have an idea of how much of your product you will need to sell in order to earn what you need, because that is how you will judge if a product or service is worth it.

Let's say you write a book about a certain technique of painting. You price this book in such a way that you receive £2 of royalties per sale. You also give a course on the same subject that brings you £100. The thing is, you usually can only do one course per month, while the book has a steady sell rate of 100 sales per month. You make twice as much with the book than with the course, so the book is clearly more profitable. There are other factors, of course, but it will happen in your art career that you will hesitate on which project to tackle next. This kind of data can provide you with what works best.

Start with your first product or service, and write down how much you expect to make from them. That will be your starting point. Keep in mind your goal, the money you need, and strive towards it.

Let's Begin!

Congratulations, you have made the first step into becoming a Full-Time Artist! Before you go further, there are a few more things I want to talk about.

First, make sure you have the support of your family and/or partner in this adventure. This decision doesn't only impact you, it will impact them too. Making a plan together will help alleviate many obstacles and keep you motivated when you struggle.

It might be a good idea to start this as a side hustle first, to see how viable it is. The side hustle will take a lot of time though, so be prepared to shuffle your time management. It might have negative consequences for your social life or even your day job, so make sure you don't burn all bridges.

Alternatively, you can jump right into the deep end like I did, if you have enough savings to catch you if you fail — because failing is a serious possibility. A lot of people don't make it at first as self-employed or business owners. Make sure you have a safety net, just in case.

Finally, remember that the distance between your dreams and reality is called "action". Take the first step towards your business, any step, even a small one, and you'll be that much closer to becoming a Full-Time Artist.

The Part-Time Artist

CHAPTER EIGHT
BEING HAPPY

Being Happy Now

The Merriam-Webster dictionary defines happiness as follows:

<u>Happiness</u>
Noun
A state of well-being and contentment.

Happiness sometimes seems unattainable for us artists. It's like we have to wait a long time until we are successful to be happy.

So many artists live in a state of transition, where they wait to experience crucial steps in their lives because they haven't made it yet. Relationships, children, travels, experiences — this transition can take years, even decades. So, should you wait all that time before you allow yourself to be happy?

I used to think that it didn't matter if I was miserable now. I had my grand master plan, I had work to do and no time to waste. I was going to be happy later, after I graduated, after I found a job, after I changed career, after I moved to the UK, after I found a new flat. There was always a reason to postpone happiness, because there was always more work to do.

If you are not careful, you can live your whole life in this waiting state, never allowing yourself to be happy, always chasing the next big project. Ambition is one thing, but learning to appreciate what you have right here and now is also important. Life will move on, whether you want it to or not. You might meet the right person before you get famous. You might become a parent while your big project is unfinished. You might be forced out of a job or place, and fall into a different experience.

"Life is what happens to you when you're busy making other plans." — John Lennon, Beautiful Boy (Darling Boy).

Yes, you have work to do, but don't neglect your happiness right now. Otherwise, one day you'll look back and wonder if all that work was worth it, compared to everything you have missed in the meantime.

KEEP THE SPARK

There will be times in your artistic career when you will be tempted to give up; to live a "normal life" and get rid of the obligations that come with your artistic tendencies. We all go through these times.

What do you do if, no matter how much effort you put into your art, you still don't get a break? What do you do if you suddenly get new responsibilities and art doesn't feel as important anymore? What do you do if you don't love your art the way you used to do?

It is OK to feel that way. Life is long and we change cyclically. We become a different person, over and over, every month, year, or decade. What you love today might not be what fulfils you in five years. What you could handle in your twenties might become unbearable in your thirties. Change is natural, and I think that fighting it is pointless. Success doesn't come from battling yourself. Success comes from being in complete alignment with who you are at this moment. Your creations might change, and you've got to change with them.

I've seen actors not make it in their twenties and give up, bitterly, after that. On the other hand, I've seen other actors in the same situation channelling their energy into a different form of creation and becoming successful in that field. I've seen people only find their "thing" after retirement.

It doesn't matter how old you are when you read this book. You haven't failed, you are on your journey and your work is important.

So if you feel like giving up, take a break, re-assess, make changes if necessary, and see if it sparks another kind of creativity.

GIVE BACK

You are not alone on your journey. Plenty of artists go through the same things, the same questions. Some will be further along their path, some will be less far than you. In this configuration, you have two choices. You can treat this as a race, work for yourself and aim to pass in front of everyone; or you can treat this as a team sport and help others on your way.

I strongly believe that we don't make it to the top by being selfish. Success does not come in a finite quantity, there's enough for everyone. Art doesn't have to be competitive, it is plentiful and infinite. You can be the spark that ignites someone's imagination. You can pick someone up from their darkest day. You can be someone's mentor, model or muse.

"A rising tide lifts all boats." — *John Fitzgerald Kennedy*

I am convinced that giving back to your community of creatives is as important as creating yourself. Nurturing talent, assisting someone who is struggling, giving someone good advice, are only a few ways you can give back. Feed creativity. Adopt a mindset of abundance instead of scarcity.

We are all in this together.

CONCLUSION

Thank you for joining me on this adventure. I hope that you found this book helpful and that it helped you on your artistic journey.

Now it's your turn to shine! Create, have fun. It is not a waste of time, and it is not a useless hobby. You've picked up this book for a reason: because you feel deep down that art is your calling. Don't ignore your intuition!

I hope that by now you believe that there is a way to be an artist no matter your circumstances. Be brave, be an example, and more importantly, be happy.

The Part-Time Artist

GOING FURTHER

Since I wrote this book, The Part-Time Artist website has grown with tons of articles and tips for your artistic career:

theparttimeartist.com

I have also created a podcast:

theparttimeartist.com/podcast

You can find me on social media at @CelineTerranova (Twitter, Instagram, Pinterest, LinkedIn). You can also send me an email directly:

info@theparttimeartist.com

And finally:

Being an independent author means that I rely on your reviews to get the book noticed by other potential readers. **I would really appreciate it if you took the time to post a review on your favourite retailer website (Amazon, Kobo, B&N…) and on Goodreads.**

Feel free to publicise it on social media, and don't hesitate to tag me into our post. If you think that my book helped you on your journey as an artist, please let others know.

ACKNOWLEDGEMENTS

A book is never truly written alone. Along the way, I was very fortunate to receive help, advice and encouragements from incredible individuals. I could not have done this without them, which is why I would like to express my gratitude to:

Eirik Knutsvik, for believing in me and in this project from the beginning, for never thinking my ideas are too bold or too crazy, and for supporting me every step of the way.

My friends and family, in Belgium and in the UK. I feel so privileged to have you all in my life!

My editors, Vicky Brewster and Abigail E. Mann, for their fantastic work on this book.

My illustrator, Juan Carlos Porcel, for his extraordinary translation of my words into visuals.

I would also like to thank all the artists who took part in the Part-Time Artist survey and interviews, in particular Joseph O'Reilly, Lauren Shields and Wayne Burke.

Finally, this book would not have been possible without the support of the writing community on Twitter. You rock!

RESOURCES

I have compiled a list of resources that might help you in your artist life. I've read / listened to / watched all of them and I recommend them!

On Being an Artist:
- Big Magic, by Elizabeth Gilbert
- Dreamer's Disease, Podcast
- Jake Parker, Youtube Channel

On Motivation and Habits:
- The Power of Habit, by Charles Duhigg
- The Slight Edge, by Jeff Olson
- Tony Robbins, Youtube Channel
- r/selfimprovement, Reddit Community
- r/NonZeroDay, Reddit Community

On Mental Health and Happiness:
- Being Happy!, by Andrew Matthews
- Touched with Fire, by Kay Redfield Jamison
- Courage & Spice, Podcast

On Money and Jobs:
- Career Change, by Joanna Penn
- Secrets of the Millionaire Mind, by T. Harv Eker
- The Richest Man in Babylon, by George S. Clason
- Quit Happens, Podcast
- The Smart Passive Income, Podcast

On Business:
- The $100 Startup, by Chris Guillebeau
- The 4-Hour Work Week, by Timothy Ferris
- How to Win Friends and Influence People, by Dale Carnegie
- StartUp Diary, Podcast
- How I Built This, Podcast

On Writing:
- How to Make a Living with your Writing, by Joanna Penn
- Helping Writers Become Authors, Podcast
- The Creative Penn, Podcast

Made in the USA
Monee, IL
30 December 2019